Breton Grammar

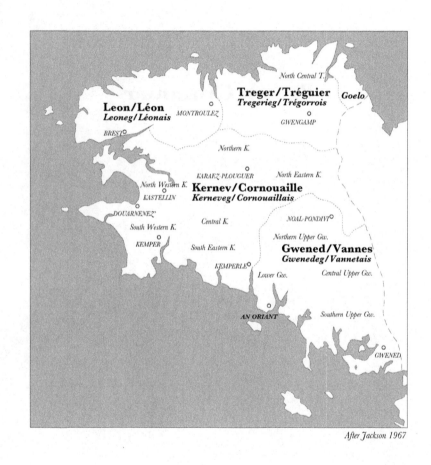

Leon/Léon
Leoneg/Léonais

MONTROULEZ

BREST

Treger/Tréguier
Tregerieg/Trégorrois

North Central T.

Goelo

GWENGAMP

Northern K.

KARAEZ-PLOUGUER

North Eastern K.

North Western K.

Kernev/Cornouaille
Kerneveg/Cornouaillais

KASTELLIN

DOUARNENEZ

South Western K.

Central K.

NOAL-PONDIVI

Northern Upper Gw.

KEMPER

South Eastern K.

Gwened/Vannes
Gwenedeg/Vannetais

KEMPERLE

Lower Gw.

Central Upper Gw.

AN ORIANT

Southern Upper Gw.

GWENED

After Jackson 1967

ROPARZ HEMON

Breton Grammar

Third English-language Edition

Translated, adapted, and revised by

Michael Everson

evertype

2011

Trugarez' da Alan Stivell evit bez'añ
roet din ar c'hoant da zeskiñ brezhoneg.

Published by Evertype, Cnoc Sceichín, Leac an Anfa, Cathair na Mart, Co. Mhaigh Eo, Éire. *www.evertype.com.*

Third edition 2011.

A catalogue record for this book is available from the British Library.

ISBN-10 1-904808-71-9
ISBN-13 978-1-904808-71-8

Typeset in Baskerville by Michael Everson.

Cover design by Michael Everson. Photograph of the Pors Kamor lighthouse, Ploumanac'h, by "Gregor69".

Printed and bound by LightningSource.

iv

TABLE OF CONTENTS

INTRODUCTION

The first English-language edition of this *Breton Grammar* was published in 1995. The book is for the most part a straightforward translation of the ninth edition of Roparz Hemon's *Grammaire bretonne*. In preparing the translation, a number of sections in the grammar were changed for the benefit of the English-speaking reader. Many, but not all, of these additions may be found in the notes to the various sections.

Some of these differences are terminological. For instance, the term "conjugated preposition" has been preferred to "prepositional pronoun" and "verbal noun" to "infinitive". The verbal and prepositional paradigms have been reorganized and altered to make them clearer; in the table following §186, for example, the delineation of the prepositional conjugations in Kervella (1976) has been followed.

More substantially, much of the section on the pronunciation of Breton, especially the phonology, has been revised in response to the needs of the English-speaking reader. In restructuring the detailed analysis of Breton phonology, particularly that of the vowel system, synthesis has been made of the best of Jackson (1967), Kervella (1976) Trépos (1980), Favereau (1992); Lagadeg and Menard (1995) has been indispensible. For the difficult question of the consonants, see the Note to §219. The International Phonetic Alphabet is used quite strictly throughout this book. As this is a teaching as well as a reference grammar, the spirit of Hemon's remarks in §§206–09 has been followed in standardizing the description and transcriptions. It is hoped that the reader first learning Breton will be served by such standardization in preparation for encountering real Breton dialects.

The reader is asked to note the use of **-z'-** in this book to indicate the orthographic **-z-** that is not pronounced in many areas (see §224), and to note that some Gwenedeg pronunciations are indicated (e.g. [gwiːʁ]/[ɥɥiːʁ]; see §208).

A bibliography has been added at the end of the book.

Thanks are due to Ronan Huon for his permission to publish this work in 1995, and to Henry Leperlier and Jean-Michel Picard, for their assistance in its preparation. I am also indebted to Maurice Jouanno, who spent many hours with me discussing Breton dialects, and to Albert Bock, who provided some splendid notes as I was preparing the second edition. I am particularly grateful to Pêr Denez, and to my friend and colleague Nicholas Williams, both of whom read the whole manuscript and made many valuable suggestions.

Michael Everson
Westport 2011

THE MUTATIONS

1. In Breton, the initial consonant of a word can change. Examples: **tad** 'father'; **va zad** 'my father'; **da dad** 'your father'.

Only eight consonants are affected by these mutations:
- the three voiceless stops: **k**, **t**, **p**;
- the four voiced stops: **g**, **gw**, **d**, **b**;
- one nasal: **m**.

2. The mutations are divided into four groups:

GROUP I: *THE HARD MUTATION*

glin 'knee'	**ho klin** 'your knee'
dant 'tooth'	**ho tant** 'your tooth'
breur 'brother'	**ho preur** 'your brother'

GROUP II: *THE SPIRANT MUTATION*

kador 'chair'	**va c'hador** 'my chair'
tal 'forehead'	**va zal** 'my forehead'
penn 'head'	**va fenn** 'my head'

GROUP III: *THE SOFT MUTATION*

kador 'chair'	**da gador** 'your chair'
tal 'forehead'	**da dal** 'your forehead'
penn 'head'	**da benn** 'your head'
glin 'knee'	**da c'hlin** 'your knee'
gwele 'bed'	**da wele** 'your knee'
dant 'tooth'	**da zant** 'your tooth'
breur 'brother'	**da vreur** 'your brother'
mamm 'mother'	**da vamm** 'your mother'

GROUP IV: *THE MIXED MUTATION*

gortoz 'wait for'	**o c'hortoz** 'waiting'
gwelout 'see'	**o welout** 'seeing'
dont 'come'	**o tont** 'coming'
bevañ 'live'	**o vevañ** 'living'
mont 'go'	**o vont** 'going'

Note: With regard to the soft and mixed mutations, note that the words beginning with *gw-* are treated differently from those beginning with *g-*.

Words beginning with *gou-* followed by a vowel can be included in the same group as words beginning with *gw-*; for example, *gouelañ* 'cry', *o ouelañ* 'crying'. But this rule is not absolute, as in *gouarn* 'govern', where *o c'houarn* 'governing' is generally found.

3. The hard mutation (Group I) occurs after the following words:

> **az'**, **ez'**, **'z'** 'you (thee)'
> **ez** 'in your (in thy)'
> **da'z'** 'to your (to thy)'
> **ho** 'your'

4. The spirant mutation (Group II) occurs after the following words:

he 'her'	**pevar** 'four' (masc.)
nav 'nine'	**teir** 'three' (fem.)
o 'their'	**tri** 'three' (masc.)
peder 'four' (fem.)	**va** 'my'

Note I: A consonant involving a flow of breath is called spirant or continuant. Hence the name spirant mutation, where a plosive or stop consonant, such as *t-*, is transformed into a spirant or continuant.

Note II: The spirant mutation does not always occur after the numerals *tri, teir* 'three', *pevar, peder* 'four', and *nav* 'nine'. Indeed it is hardly met with outside the written language. The spoken language employs the soft mutation, as indicated in the following table:

	written language	**spoken language**
kador 'chair'	*teir c'hador*	*teir gador*
tro 'turn, circuit'	*teir zro*	*teir dro*
penn 'head'	*tri fenn*	*tri benn*

5. The soft mutation (Group III) occurs after the following words:

a verbal particle	**en ur** 'while, by'
a 'of, from'	**ez'** verbal particle
aba 'since'	**hanter** 'half'
da 'at, to, for'	**holl** 'all'

da 'your (thy)'
daou 'two' (masc.)
dindan 'under'
div 'two' (fem.)
diwar 'from, because of'
dre 'through, across'
e 'his'
eme 'says, said'
endra 'while'
en em reflexive particle

na negative particle
ne negative particle
pa 'when, as; if'
pe 'or'
pe 'what?'
ra verbal particle
re 'too'
re 'those, ones'
seul 'all the more'
tra 'while, whereas'
war 'on'

Note: On occasion the expected mutation fails to occur after certain of these words, namely: *dindan* 'under', *diwar* 'from', *ez'* verbal particle, *pe* 'or', *war* 'on'.

6. The mixed mutation (Group IV) occurs after the following words:

> **e** verbal particle
> **ma** 'if' (conjunction)
> **o** verbal particle

DEFECTIVE MUTATIONS

7. Some words are followed by defective or incomplete mutations. They can be divided into four groups.

8. The first of these groups includes the words **am**, **em**, **'m** 'me', **em** 'in my', and **da'm** 'to my'. They cause the spirant mutation of **k-** and of **t-**:

kambr 'room'
ti 'house'

em c'hambr 'in my room'
em zi 'in my house'

9. The second of these groups includes the definite article, the indefinite article, and the word **hor** 'our'. After the definite article **ar** 'the' and the indefinite article **ur** 'a, an', the initial **k-** of certain nouns becomes **c'h-**.

kastell 'castle'
kazeg 'horse'

ar c'hastell 'the castle'
ar c'hazeg 'the horse'

3

Breton Grammar

The nouns affected are masculine singular nouns, and also plural nouns of either gender, with the exception of masculine nouns designating people.

Note: It is important to note that the *k- > c'h-* rule applies to all singular masculine nouns whether they designate persons, animals, or things: *kenderv* 'cousin', *ar c'henderv* 'the cousin'; *kilhog* 'cock, rooster', *ur c'hilhog* 'a cock, a rooster'; *karr* 'car', *ar c'harr* 'the car'.

In the plural, it applies to all nouns *except* masculines designating people: *kilheien* 'cocks, roosters', *ar c'hilheien* 'the cocks, the roosters'; *kirri* 'cars', *ar c'hirri* 'the cars'; *kenitervezed* 'female cousins', *ar c'henitervezed* 'the female cousins'.

After **hor**, an initial **k-** is always mutated to **c'h-**:

karr 'car'	**hor c'harr** 'our car'
kirri 'cars'	**hor c'hirri** 'our cars'
klevout 'hear'	**hor c'hlevout** 'hear us'

10. The third group includes both the definite and the indefinite article. After the definite article **ar** or **an** 'the' and the indefinite article **ur** or **un** 'a, an', nouns are subject to the soft mutation—except those which begin with **d-**:

kador 'chair'	**ar gador** 'the chair'
taol 'table'	**an daol** 'the table'
paner 'basket'	**ar baner** 'the basket'
gavr 'goat'	**ur c'havr** 'a goat'
gwern 'mast'	**ur wern** 'a mast'
bleunienn 'flower'	**ur vleunienn** 'a flower'
mamm 'mother'	**ur vamm** 'a mother'

This rule applies to almost all singular feminine nouns, such as the nouns in the table above; it also applies to plural masculine nouns designating people:

kigerien 'butchers'	**ar gigerien**
tud 'people'	**an dud**
pesketaerien 'fishermen'	**ar besketaerien**
Gallaoued 'Frenchmen'	**ar C'hallaoued**
gwerzherien 'sellers'	**ar werzherien**
breudeur 'brothers'	**ar vreudeur**
mistri 'masters'	**ar vistri**

The nouns of this category (that is singular feminine nouns and plural masculine nouns designating people) in turn mutate their adjective, provided that these nouns end in a **vowel**, or in **-l**, **-m**, **-n**, or **-r**:

kaer 'beautiful'	**ur gador gaer** 'a beautiful chair'
tev 'thick'	**ur wern dev** 'a thick mast'
paour 'poor'	**ur vamm baour** 'a poor mother'
glas 'blue'	**ar baner c'hlas** 'the blue basket'
gwenn 'white'	**ar vleunienn wenn** 'the white flower'
brudet 'famous'	**mistri vrudet** 'famous masters'
mat 'good'	**breudeur vat** 'good brothers'

11. Adjectives which follow nouns ending in a **consonant** other than **-l**, **-m**, **-n**, or **-r** are also subject to the soft mutation; but only those adjectives which begin with **g-**, **gw-**, **b-**, and **m-** (see §13). These are classed in a fourth group:

glas 'blue'	**ur voest c'hlas** 'a blue box'
gwenn 'white'	**ar gazeg wenn** 'the white mare'
brudet 'famous'	**tud vrudet** 'famous people'
mat 'good'	**ur vaouez vat** 'a good woman'

Note I: Past participles, after a noun, act like adjectives. *Brudet* 'famous, reknowned' is in fact the past participle of the verb *brudañ* celebrate'; in the preceding examples it has therefore been included among the adjectives.

Note II: Similarly, when a noun follows another noun, acting as an adjective, it is treated as a real adjective: *koad* 'wood' *un daol goad* 'a wooden table'; *Breizh* 'Brittany', *tud Vreizh* 'the Breton people'.

Note III: When a noun is followed by a number of adjectives, generally speaking it is only the first adjective is subject to mutation (if it *can* be mutated). One says *ur gazeg wenn kaer* 'a beautiful white mare'; but one can also say *ur gazeg wenn gaer*. It is important to note that after the conjunction *ha* 'and' no mutation occurs: *ur gazeg wenn ha kaer* 'a white and beautiful mare'.

Note IV: Let us suppose that a noun, instead of being followed, is preceded by an adjective.

In this case, the noun may be subject to mutation. This will be an incomplete mutation of the third type if the adjective ends in a *vowel,* or in *-l, -m, -n,* or *-r: berr* 'short', *komzoù* 'words', *e berr gomzoù* 'in few words'.

It will be an incomplete mutation of the fourth type if the adjective ends in a *consonant* other than *-l, -m, -n,* or *-r: brizh* 'bad' (when preceding a noun), *brezhoneg* 'Breton', *brizh vrezhoneg* 'bad Breton'.

But the adjective also can be subject to mutation. If it is preceded by an article, it will be subject to the mutation as if it were an integral part of the noun. Thus, *amzer* 'weather' is feminine. The adjective *gwall* 'bad' must precede it. One says *ar wall amzer* 'the bad weather', for *gwall amzer* is considered as forming a whole, in this case a feminine singular noun. It is because of this that *gwallamzer* is sometimes written as a single word.

Ti 'house' is masculine. The adjective *kozh* 'old' before a noun means 'bad'; *kozh ti* 'bad house'; *ti* is not subject to a mutation, *kozh* ending in a consonant other than *-l, -m, -n,* or *-r;* but if the indefinite article is used, for example, one says *ur c'hozh ti* 'an old house'; *k-* is subject to mutation (§9) as if *kozh ti* formed a whole.

Comparative and superlative adjectives, when they precede a noun, never cause it to mutate; but they are subject to mutation after the article: *gwellañ* 'better', *paotr* 'boy', *maouez* 'woman'; *ar gwellañ paotr* 'the better boy': the *p-* of *paotr* remains unchanged; *ar wellañ maouez* 'the better woman': the *m-* of *maouez* remains unchanged, but the *gw-* in *gwellañ* becomes *w-*, because *maouez* is feminine.

MUTATIONS IN COMPOUND WORDS

12. Many prefixes cause the root which follows them to be subject to the soft mutation (§2): **tudañ** 'populate', **didudañ** 'depopulate'.

Any word acting as a prefix also generally causes this mutation: **morvleiz'** 'shark', from **mor** 'sea' and **bleiz'** 'wolf'.

Note: The question of mutations after prefixes is a complex one, which one cannot treat in an elementary work such as this. Here, for reference, is a list of the most usual prefixes and the mutations which follow them:

AD, indicates repetition; acts for the most part only on *b-* and *m-*: *bevañ* 'live', *advevañ* 'live again'; *moger* 'wall', *advoger* 'inner wall'; acts sometimes on *g-* and *gw-*: *goulenn* 'ask', *adc'houlenn* or *adgoulenn* 'ask again'; *gwelout* 'see', *adwelout* or *adgwelout* 'see again'.

AM, indicates a negation; generally softens: *dereat* 'acceptable', *amzereat* 'improper'.

AR, various senses; generally softens: *glas* 'blue', *arc'hlas* 'bluish'.

ARALL, 'other'; generally softens: *bro* 'country', *arallvro* 'from another country'.

ARC'H, 'arch-'; does not cause mutation: *beleg* 'priest', *arc'hbeleg* 'archpriest'.

AZ, indicates repetition; does not cause mutation: *goulenn* 'ask', *azgoulenn* 'ask again'.

DAM, 'almost'; generally softens: *digor* 'open', *damzigor* 'half-open'.

DAS, DAZ, 'indicates repetition at intervals; does not cause mutation: *troc'hañ* 'cut', *dastroc'hañ* 'interrupt'.

DE, indicates approach; always softens: *kas* 'send', *degas* 'bring'.

DI, privative; always softens; *tamall* 'reproach', *didamall* 'without reproach'.

DINDAN, 'under'; generally softens: *douar* 'earth', *dindanzouar* 'underground'.

DIS, privative; may affect *g-*, *gw-*, *b-*, and *m-*: *graet* 'made', *disc'hraet* 'unmade, rumpled'; *gwel* 'seen', *diswel* or *disgwel* 'invisible'; *boued* 'food', *disvoued* 'starving'.

DREIST, 'beyond'; usually does not cause mutation; but may soften *gw-*, *b-*, and *m-*: *gwelerezh* 'view', *dreistwelerezh* or *dreistgwelerezh* 'double view'; *bec'hiañ* 'load, charge', *dreistvec'hiañ* 'overload, surcharge'; *muzul* 'measure', *dreistvuzul* 'without measure'.

DROUK, 'bad'; usually softens *g-*, *gw-*, *d-*, *b-*, and *m-*: *graet* 'made', *droukc'hraet* 'ill-made'; *gwiskañ* 'clothe', *droukwiskañ* 'deck out, dress up'; *diskred* 'mistrust', *droukziskred* 'distrust'; *berzh* 'success', *droukverzh* 'failure'; *meskañ* 'mix', *droukveskañ* 'confuse'.

EIL, 'second'; generally does not cause mutation: but may affect *gw-* and *m-*: *gouenn* 'race' *eilouenn* 'secondary race', *gou-* being here assimilated to *gw-* (see Note to §2); *maer* 'mayor'; *eilvaer* 'deputy mayor'.

EN, 'in'; generally does not cause mutation; but may affect *gw-*: *gwadañ* 'bleed', *enwadañ* 'cover with blood'.

ENEP, 'counter-'; generally does not cause mutation: but may affect *gw-*: *gwirionez'* 'truth', *enepwirionez'* or *enepgwirionez'* 'untruth'.

ETRE, 'inter-'; does not cause mutation: *etrevroadel* beside *etrebroadel* 'international', from *broadel* 'national' seems to be an exception.

FALS, 'false'; may affect *g-*, *gw-*, *d-*, *b-*, and *m-*: *moneiz'* 'coin', *falsvoneiz'* 'counterfeit coin'.

GOU, 'under, sub-'; always softens: *penn* 'head', *goubenner* 'pillow'.

GOUR, 'over, super-'; sometimes softens: *tad* 'father', *gourdad* 'ancestor'; sometimes, and more correctly, causes the spirant mutation: *kemenn* 'inform', *gourc'hemenn* 'command'.

Breton Grammar

HANTER, 'half, semi-'; generally softens: *digeriñ* 'open', *hanterzigeriñ* 'half-open'.

HE, indicates an idea of ease, of possibility; generally softens: *koll* 'lose', *hegoll* 'easy to lose'.

IS, 'under'; does not cause mutation, but *isvouezh* 'bass voice', from *mouezh* 'voice', is found.

KAMM, 'crooked'; generally softens: *tro* 'turn', *kammdro* 'detour'.

KEN, indicates a reunion, a parallelism; almost always affects *k*-: *karantez'* 'love', *kengarantez'* 'liking, mutual love'; always affects *t*-: *trec'hiñ* 'defeat', *kendrec'hiñ* 'convince'; almost always affects *p*-: *perc'henn* 'proprietor', *kenberc'henn* 'co-proprietor'; does not affect *g*-: *galv* 'call', *kengalv* 'mutual call'; sometimes affects *gw*-: *gwad* 'blood', *kenwad* 'of the same blood'; sometimes affects *d*-: *diskibl* 'disciple', *kenziskibl* 'fellow student'; always affects *b*- and *m*-: *breur* 'brother', *kenvreur* 'colleague'; *milin* 'mill', *kenvilin* 'communal mill'.

KENT, 'pre-', may affect *gw-*, *b-*, and *m*-: *broad* 'inhabitant of a country', *kentvroad* 'aboriginal'.

KIL, 'behind'; softens, but with exceptions: *pleg* 'fold', *kilbleg* or *kilpleg* 'bend, detour'.

KRAK, pejorative and diminutive; may affect *gw-*, *b-*, and *m*-: *bevañ* 'live', *krakvevañ* 'live from hand to mouth'.

KRENN, 'small, middle(-sized)'; generally softens: *paotr* 'boy', *krennbaotr* 'adolescent'.

LIES, 'poly-'; sometimes affects *gw-* and *m*-: *gwreg* 'wife', *lieswreg* 'polygamist'; *mouezh* 'voice', *liesvouezhiek* 'polyphonic'.

NEVEZ, 'new', generally softens *g-*, *gw-*, *b-*, and *m*-: *ganet* 'born', *nevez'c'hanet* 'newborn'.

PENN, 'principal'; generally softens: *kadour* 'warrior', *penngadour* 'war chief'.

PEUR, indicates completion of an action, always softens: *debriñ* 'eat', *peurzebriñ* 'eat up'.

PEUZ, 'almost'; generally softens *gw-*, *b-*, and *m*-: *marv* 'dead', *peuzvarv* 'nearly dead'.

RAK, 'before'; generally softens *gw-*, *b-*, and *m*-: *barn* 'judgement', *rakvarn* 'prejudice'.

TREUZ, 'through, trans-'; generally softens *gw-*, *b-*, and *m*-: *gwelus* 'visible', *treuzwelus* 'transparent'.

UN, 'uni-, mono-'; generally softens *gw-*, *b-*, and *m*-: *mouezh* 'voice', *unvouezh* 'unison'.

UNAN, 'uni-, mono-'; generally softens: *komz* 'speech', *unangomz* 'monologue'.

It is convenient to add that the numbers *daou, div* 'two', used as prefixes, cause the soft mutation. The numbers *tri, teir* 'three', *pevar, peder* 'four', and *nav* 'nine', used as prefixes cause the spirant mutation.

13. In a very general way, it can be said that a word used as a prefix tends to cause the soft mutation. The mutation is universal if the word acting as prefix ends in a **vowel**, or in the consonants **-l**, **-m**, **-n**, or **-r**. If the prefixing word ends in another consonant, the mutation is often limited to **g-**, **gw-**, **b-**, and **m-**.

SPECIAL MUTATIONS

14. Plac'h 'girl', **tadoù** 'fathers', **testoù** 'witnesses', **tudoù** 'peoples', **priedoù** 'spouses' do not mutate after the article.

> *Note:* Thus one says *ur plac'h* 'a girl'; but if this word is followed by an adjective, the ordinary rule of mutation (§11) is followed relative to adjectives: *ur plac'h vat* 'a good girl', from *mat* 'good'.
> The same is not true of other nouns, *tadoù, testoù, tudoù,* and *priedoù,* which are plural masculines designating people. The adjective which follows them is not subject to mutation: *tadoù mat* 'good fathers'.

15. Dor 'door' becomes **nor** after the article; **mein** 'stones' sometimes becomes **vein** after the article: **an nor**, **ar vein**.

16. Mad 'good, benefit' becomes **vad** when it is a direct object of the verb **ober** 'do, make': **an aer a ra vad d'ar yec'hed** 'the air is good for the health'.

In the same conditions **man** 'semblance, pretence' becomes **van**: **ober van** 'pretend'.

17. The word **bloaz'** 'year' is subject to a special mutation: after the numerals, except for **ur** 'one', **tri** 'three', **pevar** 'four', **pemp** 'five', and **nav** 'nine', it becomes **vloaz'**: **tregont vloaz'** 'thirty years'.

The same mutation occurs after **pet** 'how many': **pet vloaz'?** 'how many years?'.

18. From the point of view of the mutations, **tra** 'thing' acts like a feminine, though it is otherwise treated as a masculine: **un dra vat** 'a good thing'.

19. An adjective following a proper noun can be subject to mutation as though following a feminine noun: **Yann vras** 'Big John', from **bras** 'big'.

Note: This extends to some common nouns designating people: *vikel-vras* 'grand-vicar'; *laer-vor* 'pirate', lit. thief (*laer*) of the sea (*mor*)'.

OBSTACLES TO THE MUTATIONS

20. It is apparent from the above that the mutations do not occur uniformly. The behaviour of the prefixes in this respect is striking.

An important principle should be stated here: anything which tends to distance a word from the word which follows it impedes the mutation in the latter word.

For example, one says **ur stêr vras** 'a large river'; the noun **stêr** 'river' being feminine, the adjective **bras** 'large' which follows it is subject to mutation (§10). One can also say **ur stêr vras he genou** 'a river having a large mouth', lit. 'a river large its mouth'. But in this case, one can just as well say **ur stêr bras he genou**. The reason is this: even though **bras he genou** constitutes a real adjective in relation to **stêr**, and logically should be subject to mutation, its length on the one hand, and the fact that the sense of **bras** is associated more with **genou** than with **stêr**, somehow distances **bras** from **stêr** and obstructs the mutation.

In the same way, one can say **ur stêr vras-meurbet** 'a very large river', lit. 'a river large greatly'. But one can also say **ur stêr bras-meurbet**, for an analogous reason.

THE ARTICLE

21. The definite article is **al**, **an**, **ar**; the indefinite article **ul**, **un**, **ur**. The form used depends exclusively upon the initial *sound* of the word following the article:

Al and **ul** is used before **l**-; **an** and **un** before **n**-, **d**-, **t**-, **h**-, and vowels; **ar** and **ur** in other instances. Examples: **al loar** 'the moon', **an oc'hen** 'the oxen', **ur maen** 'a stone'.

Note I: English speakers are familiar with this kind of alternation: *the* is pronounced [ðə] before a consonant, and [ði:] before a vowel; *a* [ə] or [ˈeɪ] is used before consonants, and *an* [ən] or [ˈæn] before vowels: cf. *the horse, the elephant; a horse, an elephant.*

Note II: Breton is the only Celtic language to make regular use of an indefinite article. For the speaker of Gaelic or Welsh, this can take some getting used to.

Note III: In standard Breton the indefinite article **ul**, **un**, **ur** is pronounced [œl œn œʁ], as in Leoneg. In Kerneveg the pronunciation is [ɔl ɔn ɔʁ] and Gwenedeg [yl yn yʁ].

22. Al, **an**, and **ar** combine with the preposition **e** 'in', giving **el**, **en**, **er** 'in the'. Example: **er gambr** 'in the room'.

USE OF THE DEFINITE ARTICLE

23. When a noun has a complement, that is, is qualified by another noun which follows it, it does not usually take the article: **ti an tad** 'the house of the father'; **paotr e varc'h du** 'the boy on the black horse', lit. 'boy his black horse'.

24. Certain nouns like **kêr** 'town' and the names of meals do not usually take the definite article: **tostaat ouzh kêr** 'come into town'; **goude koan** 'after supper'.

Note: Ar gêr generally means 'at home'; *mont d'ar gêr* 'go home'; *bez'añ er gêr* 'be at home'.

25. The definite article is usually omitted before a comparative or superlative preceding a noun: **brasoc'h ti eo c'hoazh** 'it is a still larger house'; **kentañ ti a welis** 'the first house which I saw'.

26. The French partitive article *du, de la, des* is not translated into Breton. Examples: **holen** 'salt' (*du sel*), **pri** 'clay' (*de la boue*), **nadoz'ioù** 'needles' (*des aiguilles*). There is naturally exception to this where the noun is determinate: **kemeret em eus darn eus an nadoz'ioù a oa war an daol** 'I have taken some of the needles which were on the table'. (Breton and English are alike in the use of the plural without an article.)

27. As in English, the definite article is not used in some expressions, although it is found in French: **ober skol** 'hold a class' (*faire l'école*), **benañ maen** 'cut stone' (*tailler la pierre*), **war-dro noz** 'towards night, towards evening' (*vers la nuit*); but cf. **redek bro** 'roam the country' (*courir le pays*).

28. Before certain nouns expressing temporal divisions, Breton, like English, uses a preposition and the article. Examples: **diouzh ar beure** 'in the morning', meaning 'during the morning'; **diouzh an abardaez'** 'in the evening'; but note **diouzh an noz** 'at night'; **d'al lun** 'Monday', 'on Monday'; **en hañv** or **e-pad an hañv** 'in summer', 'during the summer'.

29. In some expressions where English does not use an article, Breton uses the definite article: **dec'h ar beure** 'yesterday morning'; **c'hwezh an trenk** 'a smell of acid'; **ruz'iañ gant ar vezh** 'blush with shame'.

THE DEFINITE ARTICLE BEFORE PROPER NAMES

30. Apart from the names of some rivers and certain mountains and towns, proper names do not generally take the definite article: **an Elorn** 'the Elorn', **an Alpoù** 'the Alps', **ar C'hozh-Varc'had** 'Vieux-Marché'. Compare **Breizh** 'Brittany' (*la Bretagne*), **Europa** 'Europe' (*l'Europe*).

> *Note I:* The names of countries borrowed through French take the article in popular usage: *an Itali* 'Italy' (*l'Italie*), *ar Spagn* 'Spain' (*l'Espagne*).
> *Note II:* Although in French the article is used before a proper noun accompanied by an adjective, in Breton, as in English, it is not: *Breizh nevez'* 'new Brittany' (*la nouvelle Bretagne*), *Mona goant* 'pretty Mona' (*la jolie Mona*).

31. Note the use of the article before **aotrou** 'Mister', **itron** 'Mrs', **dimezell** 'Miss' and their plurals: **an Aotrou Bizien** 'Mr Bizien', unless one is addressing the person directly: **kenavo, Aotrou Bizien** 'good bye, Mr Bizien'.

These words are not otherwise followed by the article, as they would be in French: **an Aotrou Kannad** 'the Deputy' (in address, 'Deputy'; *Monsieur le Député*), **an Itron Renerez** 'the Director' (in address, 'Director'; *Madame la Directrice*). Exceptional are nouns beginning with a vowel: **an Aotrou 'n Eskob** 'his Grace the Bishop', 'the very reverend Bishop' (in address, 'my lord Bishop', 'Bishop'; *Monseigneur l'Evêque*), **an Aotrou 'n Abad** 'the Reverend Abbot' (in address, 'Father'; *Monsieur l'Abbé*). **'n** probably represents the article **an**.

> *Note I:* Note that in English terms of address are not used in the same way as in Breton (or French).
> *Note II:* The definite article may be found before a surname. But this use is more familiar and can even be pejorative: for example, when one designates someone named *Bizien* by *ar Bizien*.

32. The names of peoples and of inhabitants of regions or towns ending in **-iz** may not take the article: **Breizhiz** 'the Bretons', instead of **ar Vreizhiz**; **Kemperiz** 'the Quimpérois' instead of **ar Gemperiz**.

USE OF THE INDEFINITE ARTICLE

33. Before the nouns **miz** 'month' and **bloaz'** 'year', the indefinite article is not used: **miz 'zo** 'a month ago'; **chom a reas bloaz' e Brest** 'he stayed a year in Brest'.

34. Although French confuses the article '*un, une*' and the numeral '*un, une*', Breton makes the same distinction as does English: '*a, an*' before a noun is **ul**, **un**, or **ur**; '*one*' in isolation is **unan**. Examples: **ur gador am eus** 'I have a chair'; **unan am eus** 'I have one'.

THE NOUN

GENDER

35. Breton has two genders: masculine and feminine.

36. Masculine nouns are nouns which refer to male human beings, male animals, and most objects, in particular nouns in **-adur**, except for **plijadur** 'pleasure' and the abstract nouns in **-der** and in **-erezh**.

37. Feminine nouns are nouns which refer to female human beings, female animals, most geographical nouns (countries, towns, rivers) and some things, in particular most nouns in **-ez**, in **-ezh** (except the abstract nouns in **-erezh**), in **-enn**, in **-ell**, in **-ded**, and abstract nouns in **-i**.

38. A feminine suffix **-ez** is added to masculines: **ki** 'dog', **kiez** 'bitch'.

Note I: As in other languages, it often happens that the feminine is indicated by a completely different word from the masculine: *tad* 'father', *mamm* 'mother'; *eontr* 'uncle', *moereb* 'aunt'; *paotr* 'boy', *plac'h* 'girl'; *tarv* 'bull', *buoc'h* 'cow', etc. Note that alongside *plac'h*, there is a feminine *paotrez*, though this is sometimes used pejoratively.

Note II: The suffix *-enn* serves sometimes, though rarely, to form feminines: *krennard* 'adolescent' has for feminines *krennardenn* or *krennardez*. It is often used to form familiar feminine proper names: along with *Plougastelladez* 'woman from Plougastel', the more familiar form *Plougastellenn* is found. Note also the use of *-enn* as an ending serving to form feminine nouns of persons: *pebrenn* 'shrewish woman', from *pebr* 'pepper'; *koantenn* 'pretty girl', from *koant* 'pretty'.

Note III: For certain animals, the sex is designated with the aid of *tad* 'father' and *mamm* 'mother' placed before the noun: *un tad golvan* 'a male sparrow'. The prefix *tar* is also found, doubtless derived from *tarv* 'bull': *targazh* 'tomcat'.

39. The word **tra** is considered neuter (see §18).

SINGULAR AND PLURAL

40. The plural is generally formed:

a) by adding **-où** or **-ioù** to nouns referring to things: **lenn** 'lake', **lennoù**; **taol** 'table', **taolioù**;

b) by adding **-ed** to nouns referring to persons, animals, trees: **merc'h** 'girl', **merc'hed**; **pesk** 'fish', **pesked**; **avalenn** 'apple tree', **avalenned**.

41. Some nouns referring to persons take **-où**: **testoù** 'witnesses'; likewise the word **leue** 'calf', **leueoù**.

42. The plural is also marked by other endings: **-i**, **-ier**, **-ien**, **-on**, **-ez**, **-en**, etc.; the root vowel of the singular is frequently altered before them: **bran** 'crow', **brini**; **arc'h** 'chest', **irc'hier**; **eskob** 'bishop', **eskibien**; **gad** 'hare', **gedon**; **ti** 'house', **tiez**; **draf** 'little gate', **drefen**.

43. Sometimes a change of the singular vowel is sufficient: **dant** 'tooth', **dent**.

44. Following are some interesting special cases:

a) Nouns referring to human beings in **-ad** generally form their plural in **-idi**, or in **-iz** if they indicate inhabitants of countries, towns, etc.: **lazhiad** 'victim', **lazhidi**; **Breizhad** 'Breton', **Breizhiz**;

b) Nouns referring to human beings in **-er** and **-our** generally form their plural in **-erien** and **-ourien**: **kiger** 'butcher', **kigerien**; **oberour** 'author', **oberourien**. Sometimes one finds **-erion** and **-ourion**;

c) Nouns referring to human beings in **-eg** often form their plural in **-eien**: **gouizieg** 'scholar', **gouizieien**. Sometimes **-eion** is used.

45. Many plurals are irregular. Note the following: **den** 'person', **tud**; **ki** 'dog', **kon** or **chas**; **marc'h** 'horse', **mirc'hed** or **kezeg**; **ejen** 'ox', **ejened** or **oc'hen**; **buoc'h** 'cow', **saout** 'cows, cattle'; a plural of **buoc'h** in a more restrained sense is **buoc'henned** (also **buoc'hed**, **bioù** 'cattle').

46. Note the diminutives which are formed by adding **-ig** to the singular and **-igoù** in the plural: **ti**, **tiig** 'house, cottage'; **tiez**, **tiezigoù** 'houses, cottages'; **bag**, **bagig** 'boat, little boat', **bagoù**, **bagoùigoù** 'boats, little boats'. **Tud** has a plural diminutive **tudigoù** 'unimportant people'.

COLLECTIVE AND SINGULATIVE

47. Certain nouns have a collective sense, in that they refer to a group of objects, or to a class of objects (materials, animals, plants, etc.).

To express the idea of one of these objects in isolation or of a member of the group, the ending **-enn** is added: **geot** 'herb', **geotenn** 'sprig of herb'; **gwez'** 'trees', **gwez'enn** 'tree'; **kouevr** 'copper', **kouevrenn** 'piece of copper'. All of these nouns in **-enn** are feminine.

48. These singulatives act like singulars: **geotennoù** 'sprigs of herb'.

Note: Penn 'head' or *loen* 'animal' before a plural also sometimes form a kind of singulative: *ur penn-deñved* 'a (head of) sheep', from *deñved* 'sheep'; *ul loen-kezeg* 'a horse', from *kezeg* 'horses'. Note *pemoc'h* 'pig', from *moc'h* 'pigs'.

THE DUAL

49. Nouns referring to the double organs of the body generally have a dual, or special plural formed with the aid of **daou-** for masculines, and of **di-** or **div-** for feminines: **lagad** 'eye', **an daoulagad** 'the (two) eyes; **skouarn** 'ear', **an diskouarn**, **an divskouarn** 'the (two) ears'.

Note I: These words in turn may be pluralized: *daoulagadoù* 'pairs of eyes'.

Note II: Words such as *lagad, skouarn*, etc., when they do not designate the organs of the body, have an ordinary plural: *lagadoù* 'eyes (as spots of grease on the surface of a liquid)'; *skouarnoù* 'handles (of vases)'.

Note III: Note the irregular forms: *glin* 'knee', *an daoulin* 'the (two) knees'; *dorn* 'hand', *an daouarn* 'the (two) hands'; *gar* 'leg', *an divhar* 'the (two) legs'.

DOUBLE PLURALS

50. The word **tud** 'people' has a plural **tudoù**, which is identical in meaning to **tud**, but is imployed more familiarly. **Dilhad** 'clothes' likewise has a plural **dilhadoù**.

51. Along with some plurals in **-où** or in **-ioù**, there are plurals in **-eier**, in a more general sense, and which can be considered as double plurals: **parkoù** 'fields', **parkeier** 'fields, open country'; **koadoù** 'woods', **koadeier** 'woods, forests in general'; **edoù** 'flour', **edeier** 'wheats, cereals'.

Note: In this category can be included: *botez* 'shoe', *botoù* 'pair of shoes', *boteier* 'shoes in general'; *bragez* 'leg of trousers', *bragoù* 'a pair of trousers', *brageier* 'trousers'.

THE GENITIVE

52. A noun can stand in genitive relation to another noun. Several types must be distinguished.

53. The genitive object can be definite. In this instance, the noun which precedes is used without an article (see §23): **tog Anna** 'Anna's hat, the hat of Anna'; **marc'h ar miliner** 'the horse of the miller'; **taol vras ar gegin** 'the big kitchen table'; **bro va zad** 'the country of my father'.

Note: Note particular expressions such as *paotr e fri hir* 'the boy with the long nose', lit. 'boy his long nose'; *plac'h he blev troc'het* 'the girl with cut hair', lit. 'girl her cut hair(s)'. Another example is found at §23. In this case it is also correct to use the article: *ar paotr e fri hir; ar plac'h he blev troc'het.*

54. The genitive object can be indefinite. It simply follows the noun before it, which retains the article: **an ti kenwerzh** 'the house of commerce', **un tamm kig** 'a piece of meat', **ur voestad westell** 'a box of cakes'.

Note I: In this case the two nouns can be linked by the preposition *a* 'of': *tud a youl-vat* 'people of good will', *un den a vicher* 'a craftsman'. If the first nouns is followed by an adjective, *a* is almost always used: *un tamm mat a gig* 'a good piece of meat'.
Note II: The relationship between the two nouns may be marked in a more precise manner by another preposition; for example, *eus* or *digant*, indicating provenance: *paotred eus Lesneven* 'men of Lesneven'; *ur prof digant ar roue* 'a gift of the king'; or *da*, marking or not the possession: *un niz(h) d'ar barner* 'a nephew of the judge'; or any other preposition: *an aon rak an archerien* 'the fear of the police', *un den diwar ar maez* 'a man of the countryside', *doujañs ouzh ar binvidien* 'respect for the rich'.

THE PERSONAL PRONOUN

55. As in English, the personal pronoun takes different forms depending on whether it is subject or object of the verb. The table below indicates the subject form and the direct object form:

me	I	**va, 'm**	me
te	you (thou)	**da, 'z'**	you (thee)
eñ	he	**e, hen**	him
hi	she	**he**	her
ni	we	**hol, hon, hor**	us
c'hwi	you	**ho, hoc'h**	you
i, **int**	they	**o**	them

Note: The possessive pronoun of the first person singular is *ma* in the standard language and *va* in Leoneg. The author favours the latter form throughout this book.

56. In the first person singular, the form **va** of the direct object is used before a verbal noun, past participle, or imperative (but only in the affirmative of the imperative): **va gwelout** 'see me'; **va gwelet o deus** 'they have seen me'; **va selaouit** 'listen to me'.

Before a verbal noun, however, after the preposition **da** 'for', **'m** is used: **da'm gwelout** 'to see me'.

Before the other forms of the verb, **'m** is used: **ne'm gwelas ket** 'he did not see me'; **na'm zamallit ket** 'do not blame me'; **va breur am gwelas** 'my brother saw me'; **neuze em gwelas** 'then he saw me'. Note that it is not customary to write **a'm** or **e'm**. The forms **d'am**, **n'em**, **n'am** are also often written instead of **da'm**, **ne'm**, **na'm**.

57. The same applies in the second person singular with regard to the use of **da** and **'z'**.

Examples: **Da welout** 'see you'; **da zegemeret o deus** 'they have received you'; **va breur az' kwelas** 'my brother saw you'; **da'z' kwelout** 'to see you'.

Note I: The preposition *da* and the personal pronoun *da* are two words of completely different origin and must not be confused.

Note II: In the dialects which do not pronounce *-z'-* the only difference between *da welout* and *da'z' kwelout* is the mutation.

58. In the third person singular masculine, the direct object pronoun **e** is used before the verbal noun and the past participle: **e welout** 'see him'; **e welet em eus** 'I have seen him'; **hen** is used in other instances: **ni hen gwel** 'we see him'. There is an exception in the affirmative of the imperative: see §66. **Hen** is sometimes written **en**.

59. In the third person singular feminine, the direct object pronoun **he** is used in all instances: **he gwelout** 'see her'; **he gwelet em eus** 'I have seen her'; **me he gwel** 'I see her'. But there is an exception in the affirmative of the imperative: see §66. The form **hec'h** is sometimes used instead of **he** before a vowel.

60. In the first person plural, **hol**, **hon**, and **hor** are used in exactly the same way as the article **al**, **an**, and **ar**; that is, **hol** is used before **l-**, **hon** before **n-**, **d-**, **t-**, **h-**, and vowels, and **hor** in other cases: **hol lezel** 'let us'; **hon touellañ** 'deceive us'; **hor c'havout** 'find us'.

61. In the second person plural, **ho** is used before a consonant and **hoc'h** before a vowel: **ho klevout** 'hear you'; **hoc'h aliañ** 'counsel you'.

62. In the third person plural, gender is not distinguished, as in English; **i** and **int** are used indifferently.
O is the object form, except in the affirmative of the imperative: see §66.

Note: There is another form, *int-i*, which is used to give more force to the pronoun.

63. The indirect object form of the personal pronoun is not presented in this chapter. The personal pronoun, when it is an indirect object, always follows a preposition and is realized in the prepositional conjugation.
Example: **evit** 'for', **evidon** 'for me'. For further discussion on this see the chapter on the prepositions (§§182–87).

USE OF THE PERSONAL PRONOUN

64. The subject personal pronoun is not expressed in the majority of instances. As in Latin, the form of the verb suffices to indicate the person. When the subject pronoun is expressed, it is almost always because it is stressed. In the sentence **skrivañ a rit bemdez'** 'you write every day', no pronoun is expressed. If one says **c'hwi a skriv bemdez'**, it is to stress the pronoun, and the sentence means rather 'it is *you* who write every day'.

There are two ways to introduce the subject personal pronoun in a sentence:

    a) by placing it, as in English, before the verb: **te a welo** 'you will see';

    b) by placing it immediately after the verb; in this case, the hyphen is used: **warc'hoazh e weli-te** 'tomorrow you will see'.

Note: After a verb, instead of *c'hwi* 'you', a special form, *hu*, may be used: *ne welit-hu ket?* 'don't you see?'.

65. The direct object pronoun is placed immediately before the verb: **me ho kar** 'I love you'; **me am eus ho karet** 'I have loved you'.

66. In the imperative, and only in the affirmative, the subject pronoun may be used (after the verb) instead of the direct object pronoun: **lezit me** 'let me' instead of **va lezit**. This is mandatory for the third person pronouns: **lezit eñ**, **lezit hi**, **lezit i** 'let him, let her, let them'.

67. After **setu** 'behold', the subject pronoun is used: **setu hi** 'here she is', 'behold her'.

68. When the pronoun is used in isolation, it always takes the subject form, even if logically it could be considered a direct object of the verb: **Piv a welit? Eñ** 'Whom do you see? Him'.

Note: Likewise, the subject pronoun is used in expressions like: *me eo* 'it's me', *int e oa* 'it was them'. Note that in English the object form is usually used in such expressions.

69. Except in Gwenedeg, the traditional form of the object pronoun has almost died out in speech. It has been replaced by partitive periphrasis: Kerneveg, Leoneg, and Tregerieg speakers will normally not say **me ho kar** 'I love you' or **me da wel** 'I see you' (although this is still used to some extent in a conservative literary register and some fossilized phrases), but **me a gar ac'hanout** (lit. 'I love of you') or **me a wel ac'hanout** (lit. 'I see of you'), with the conjugated preposition **a** 'of' after the verb. The original forms of the pronoun are only restored when the object fronted for emphasis, as in **te a welan!** 'I see *you*!'. 'It's *you* I see', etc. **Me ho kar** or **ho karout a ran** is the norm in Gwenedeg.

70. As in French, when addressing a single person, one may use **c'hwi** '*vous*' for politeness. The use of **te** is much the same in Breton as '*tu*' is in French, though there is a large area in central Brittany which has lost **te** entirely. See the map below.

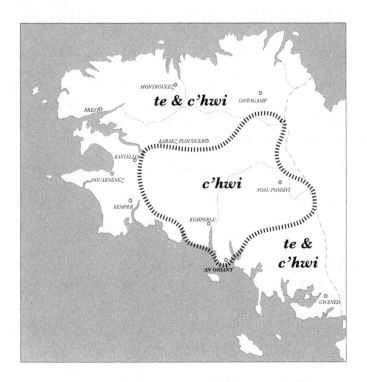

THE QUALIFYING ADJECTIVE

71. The qualifying adjective is invariable. However, **kaezh** 'poor' sometimes has a plural **keizh**. Example: **tud keizh** 'poor people'.

Note: The adjective *mez'v* 'drunk' has a feminine form, *mez'vez*: *Per a oa mezv, e wreg a oa mez'vez* 'Peter was drunk, his wife was drunk'.

DEGREES OF COMPARISON

72. The equative is formed with the aid of **ken**: **gwan** 'weak', **ken gwan** 'as weak'. It is followed by the conjunction **ha** 'and', which becomes **hag** before a vowel: **ken gwan ha ma krede** 'as weak as he believed'; **ken kreñv hag ur marc'h** 'as strong as a horse'.

Note: Expressions like 'as weak as that' are formed with the aid of the word *se*: *ken gwan-se*.
To reinforce the idea of the equative, *all* 'other' may be placed after the adjective: *ken gwan all*.

73. The comparative is formed with the aid of the ending **-oc'h**: **gwanoc'h** 'weaker'. It is followed by the conjunction **eget**: **gwanoc'h eget e vreur** 'weaker than his brother; **gwanoc'h eget ma krede** 'weaker than he believed'.

Note: Instead of *eget*, especially in colloquial Breton, *evit* is sometimes used.

74. The superlative is formed with the ending **-añ**; it is almost always preceded by the definite article (see §25): **ar gwanañ** 'the weakest'; **ar c'hezeg bravañ** 'the most beautiful horses'.
It is generally followed by the preposition **eus** 'from': **ar wez'enn uhelañ eus al liorzh** 'the tallest tree in the garden'. See also §84.

Note I: 'Of all' after a superlative is expressed by *holl*: *ar bravañ-holl* 'the most beautiful of all'.
Note II: The article is omitted in expressions like: *kentañ a reas* 'the first thing that he did'; *gwashañ oa…* 'the worst of it was that…'; *muiañ ma c'halle* 'the most that he could'.

75. Adjectives ending in **-z**, like **kriz'** 'cruel', change this **-z-** to **-s-**: **kris'oc'h**, **kris'añ**. Adjectives ending in **-zh**, like **kozh** 'old', change this **-zh-** to **-sh-**: **koshoc'h**, **koshañ**. The rare adjectives ending in **-b** or in **-d** change these consonants respectively to **-p-** and **-t-**: **gleb** 'humid', **glepoc'h**, **glepañ**; **yud** 'treacherous', **yutoc'h**, **yutañ**.

Note: See Note I at §224 below.

76. The following comparatives and superlatives are irregular: **gwell**, **gwelloc'h** 'better', **gwellañ** 'best'; **gwazh**, **gwashoc'h** 'worse', **gwashañ** 'worst'; **mui**, **muioc'h** 'more', **muiañ** 'most'; **kent**, **kentoc'h** 'before, sooner', **kentañ** 'first'.

Note I: Sometimes *ken gwazh ha* 'as bad as', *ken gwazh all* 'as bad' form the equative.

Note II: Gwell, gwelloc'h, gwellañ serve as comparatives and superlative to *mat* 'good'; *matoc'h* or *matañ* are not usually found, except in the composition *marc'had-mat* 'bargain', whose comparative is *gwelloc'h marc'had* or *marc'hadmatoc'h*, and whose superlative is *gwellañ marc'had* or *marc'hadmatañ*. (In at least one of the dialects of Gwenedeg, *matoc'h* is used for physical things like bread, and *gwellañ* for subjective things like feelings.)
Gwazh, gwashoc'h, gwashañ serve as comparatives and superlative to *fall* 'bad'; but *falloc'h* and *fallañ* also occur.

77. The comparative and superlative of inferiority can be formed with **nebeutoc'h** 'less', **nebeutañ** 'the least': **nebeutoc'h gwan** 'less weak'; **an nebeutañ gwan** 'the least weak'.

78. The past participle of verbs is inflected like an adjective as far as the comparative and superlative are concerned: **karet**, **karetoc'h**, **karetañ** 'beloved, more beloved, the most beloved'.

Note: Muioc'h and *muiañ* also occur before a past participle: *muioc'h doujet* 'more respected', *ar muiañ doujet* 'the most respected'. This formation is not to be recommended, except in the expression: *ar muiañ karet* 'the girlfriend'.

79. Note the use of **seul** 'the more': **seul vuanoc'h, seul welloc'h** 'the quicker, the better'; **seul vuioc'h ma selle, seul nebeutoc'h e wele** 'the more he that looked, the less he saw'; **deskiñ a ra seul**

welloc'h ma en deus c'hoant deskiñ 'he learns all the better because he wants to'.

80. 'More and more' is expressed with the aid of the comparative followed by the superlative: **kreñvoc'h-kreñvañ** 'stronger and stronger'. However, 'more and more' itself is formed with '**muioc'h-mui**'. Note also **gwashoc'h-gwazh**, beside **gwashoc'h-gwashañ** 'from bad to worse'.

'Less and less' is expressed by **nebeutoc'h-nebeutañ**.

One also says **mui-ouzh-mui, gwazh-ouzh-gwazh**.

THE EXCLAMATIVE

81. By replacing **-añ** by **-at** in the superlative, the exclamative is formed: **gwanat den!** or **na gwanat den!** or **na gwanat un den!** 'what a weak person!'; **koshat ti!** 'what an old house!'

THE DIMINUTIVE

82. Any adjective can have a diminutive, formed with the ending **-ik**. If the adjective ends in one of the consonants **-p, -t, -k**, or **-s**, preceded by a vowel, the consonant softens to **-b-, -d-, -g-**, or **-z-**. Examples: **bihan** 'small', **bihanik**; **bras** 'large', **brazik**. However, **-s** sometimes resists: **dous** 'soft', **dousik**.

USE OF THE QUALIFYING ADJECTIVE

83. The qualifying adjective is placed after the noun, as in Gaelic and Welsh: **un den gwan** 'a weak person'. Some exceptions to this are the adjectives like **gwall, krak**: **ur gwall spont** 'a famous fear', **ur c'hrak paotr** 'a sickly boy'.

Certain other adjectives are also placed before the noun: **kozh** 'old', **brizh** 'speckled', taken in a pejorative sense: **ur c'hozh ti** 'a miserable house', **brizh vrezhoneg** 'bad Breton'.

Hir 'long', **berr** 'short', **kaezh** 'poor', **gwir** 'true', are sometimes placed before the noun: **dre hir aked** 'through long care', **e berr gomzoù** 'in few words', **ur c'haezh paotr** 'a poor boy'; **ur wir garantez'** 'a true love'.

Note: Note the particular expressions like *ur gaer a blac'h* 'a pretty girl', where the adjective precedes the noun and is linked to it by the preposition *a* 'of', lit. 'a pretty of a girl'. French uses similar expressions: *un drôle de chapeau* 'a funny hat' in Breton is *un iskis a dog*.

84. The comparative and the superlative of the adjective are placed indifferently before or after the noun: **gwelloc'h den** or **un den gwelloc'h** 'a better person'; **ar gwanañ den**, **gwanañ den**, **an den ar gwanañ**, **an den gwanañ** 'the weakest person'.

85. Adjectives are sometimes used substantively. In such cases they behave exactly like nouns. Example: **mut** 'mute'. Taken as a noun, it is written **mud** (an orthographic rule requires that adjectives generally end in a voiceless consonant, and nouns in a voiced one); it will have a feminine and a plural: **ar mud** 'the mute', **ar vudez** 'the mute (woman)', **ar vuded** 'the mutes'.

THE POSSESSIVE

86. The possessive adjectives have exactly the same form as the direct object personal pronouns:

> **ma zi**, **va zi** 'my house'
> **da di** 'your house'
> **e di** 'his house'
> **he zi** 'her house'
> **hon ti** 'our house'
> **ho ti** 'your house
> **o zi** 'their house'

For the various forms of these adjectives, refer to the table at §55 and to the following paragraphs.

Note I: It is important to note that in Breton the possessive adjectives do not depend on the gender or number of the noun which follows, as they do in French. Just as in English, the third person singular possessive adjective agrees with the gender of the possessor.

Note II: The possessive pronoun of the first person singular is *ma* in the standard language and *va* in Leoneg. The author favours the latter form throughout this book.

87. **'m** and **'z'** are only used after the preposition **da** 'to, of': **da'm breur** 'to my brother', **da'z' preur** 'to your brother'. They also combine with the preposition **e** 'in' to give **em** and **ez**: **em c'hambr** 'in my room', **ez kambr** 'in your room'.

Note: The compound *ez* does not occur in the dialects which do not pronounce the *-z*, so *ez'* has not been written here. The forms often found are: *ez kambr* (Leoneg), *e da gambr* (Tregerieg, Kerneveg), *en da gambr* (Tregerieg), *en ha gambr* (Gwenedeg), *e ta gambr* (South Gwenedeg).

88. Breton has no possessive pronouns per se. They are supplied in the singular by the use of the word **hini**, and in the plural by the word **re**: **va hini** 'mine, my one', **va re** 'mine, my ones'.

89. Note a special way of marking the possessive: **al liv anezhañ**, lit. 'the colour of him', instead of **e liv** 'his colour'.

90. If one wishes to stress the possessive, one follows the noun which follows the possessive adjective with the corresponding subject pronoun: **va breur-me** '*my* brother', **da vreur-te** '*your* brother'.

One may also follow the noun with the preposition **da** 'to, of' conjugated in the corresponding number: **e vreur dezhañ** 'his brother of him' (cf. '*son frère à lui*').

Note: According to the same logic, one says: *ur breur din* 'a brother of mine', *ur c'hoar dezho* 'a sister of theirs'.

91. The possessive adjectives, followed by the word **unan** 'one', form compounds corresponding to the English 'yourself, yourself', etc.: **va-unan** 'myself', **hon-unan** 'ourselves'.

Note I: Va-unan, da-unan, etc. can also mean 'me alone, you alone', etc. In this sense, they are sometimes followed by the word *penn* 'head': *bez' e oamp hon-unan-penn* 'we were all alone'.

Note II: When, in the third person singular, the possessor is indefinite or undefined, one may use the word *an-unan* 'itself': *en em lakaat an-unan da varner* 'to set oneself up as a judge'.

92. The possessive adjectives combine with the numerals to form expressions corresponding to English 'we two, you three', etc.: **hon-daou** 'we two', **ho-tri** 'you three', **o-fevar** 'they four'.

93. In phrases like 'he has broken his arm', where in French the definite article is used ('*il s'est cassé le bras*'), Breton, like English, uses the possessive adjective: **terriñ a reas e vrec'h** 'he broke his arm'.

THE DEMONSTRATIVE

94. The demonstrative consists of three degrees and is formed with the aid of the definite article and a particle placed after the noun: **an den-mañ** 'this person', **an den-se** 'that person', **an den-hont** 'that person over there'.

95. If the noun is followed by an adjective, the particle follows the adjective: **an den fall-se** 'that evil person'.

96. The demonstrative pronouns are: **hemañ**, **hennezh**, **henhont** 'this one, that one, that one over there (masculine)'; **houmañ**, **hounnezh**, **hounhont** 'this one, that one, that one over there' (feminine); **ar re-mañ**, **ar re-se**, **ar re-hont** 'these, those, those over there'.

Note I: In the plural, one uses the same forms for masculine and feminine.
Note II: Compare: *amañ* 'here', *aze* 'there', *ahont* 'yonder, over there'.

97. 'This' is expressed by **an dra-mañ** lit. 'this thing'; 'that' by **an dra-se**; and 'that over there' by **an dra-hont** .

98. 'All this' is expressed by **kement-mañ**; 'all that' by **kement-se**; one may say, though it is rare, **kement-hont** 'all that over there'.

Note: On occasion the particle *se* is used by itself with the sense 'that': *se eo a lavaras* 'it is that which he said'.

99. 'This who, this which' is expressed by **ar pezh a** or simply **pezh a**. Example: **setu amañ ar pezh a reas**, or **setu amañ pezh a reas** 'this is what he did'.

100. 'That who, that which' is expressed by **an hini a**; 'those which' by **ar re a**. Examples: **kemer an hini a blij dit** 'take that which you want'; **lez ar re a zo fall** 'leave those which are bad'.

Note: More generally, one may say that 'this' followed by a relative pronoun is expressed by *ar pezh* or *pezh*; that 'that' followed by a relative pronoun is expressed by *an hini*; that 'those' followed by a relative pronoun is translated by *ar re*. Example: *an hini ma komzit anezhañ* 'that which you speak about (it)'.

'This' is also sometimes expressed by *an dra* 'the thing': *an dra ma komzit anezhañ* 'this which you speak about (it)'.

101. The use of **se** with an adjective in the equative has already been noted (see §72): **ken souezhus-se** 'as surprising as that'.

THE INTERROGATIVE

102. There exists a series of interrogative adjectives: **pe** 'what'; **peseurt**, **petore** 'what kind of'; **pet** 'how many'.

Note I: *Pe* is not used in contemporary language: one may say *pe vro?* 'what country?', but more commonly one says *peseurt bro? petore bro?*, lit. 'what kind of country?'.

Note II: After *pet* 'how many', the noun is put into the singular: *pet den?* 'how many people?'. However, one may put the preposition *a* 'of' after *pet*; in this case, the noun is put in the plural: *pet a dud?* 'how many people?'. The word *nouspet* 'no one knows how many' is used in the same way.

Note III: *Pet* has a derivative, *petvet*, which is used to ask the rank in a series or to refer to a number in a series: *ar petvet deiz' eus ar miz?* 'what day of the month?'; *petvet* is also used as a pronoun: *ar petvet?* 'which', lit. 'the how-many-eth?' (*'le quantième'*).

103. The interrogative pronouns are: **piv** 'who', **petra** 'what', **pehini** 'which one', **pere** 'which ones'.

Note: The use of these pronouns offers no difficulties. It is important to note, when translating from English, that one must not confuse them with the relative pronouns. In English, some of the interrogative pronouns have the same form as relative pronouns. 'Who', 'which', 'what' are expressed in Breton by *piv*, *petra* only when they express a direct or indirect question: *piv a zo aze?* 'who is there?'; *ne ouzon ket piv a zo aze* 'I don't know who is there'. Cf. *an den a zo o tont* 'the man who comes' with *piv a zo o tont?* 'who comes?'.

104. The interrogative adverbs are: **pegement** 'how much'; **pegeit** 'how long, how far'; **perak** 'why'; **penaos** 'how'; **peur, pegoulz, pe vare** 'when'; **pelec'h** 'where'.

Note: Pegement (cf. *pet*, §102, Note II) can be followed by *a*: *pegement a win?* 'how much wine?'

THE EXCLAMATIVE

105. The exclamative is formed with the aid of the following adjectives or adverbs: **pebezh** 'what a… [noun]!', **pegen** 'how… [adjective]!', **na**, which becomes **nag** before a vowel 'how…! what…!' (before a declaration): **pebezh den!** 'what a man!'; **pegen brav!** 'how beautiful!'; **nag a dud!** 'what a crowd!'.

Note: Refer here to §81.

THE INDEFINITE

SOME

106. The idea expressed in English by the word 'some' is expressed in Breton by the word **bennak**, which is placed after the word it relates to: **un ti bennak** 'some house, a certain house'; **ur wech bennak** 'some time, a certain time'.

Note I: Bennak often corresponds to English 'about': *ur miz a zo bennak* 'about a month ago'; *un tri c'hant bennak* 'about three hundred'.

Note II: It is also used after words like *pegen* 'as', *pegement* 'as much', *pelec'h* 'where', *petra* 'what', etc. in the sense of 'ever': *pegen dister bennak e vefe* 'as trite as he is'; *pegement bennak a garantez' en doa outi* 'as much love as he had for her'; *e pelec'h bennak e vevfemp* 'wherever we would live'; *petra bennak a lavar* 'whatever he says'.

Note III: 'Somewhere' is said *en un tu bennak*, or simply *tu bennak*.

107. Breton **an neb** corresponds to the English pronoun 'whoever'. Example: **an neb a venn, hennezh a c'hell** 'whoever is willing, (that one) can (do it)'.

108. 'Someone' is expressed by **unan bennak**; 'some' by **unan bennak** or **ur re bennak**; 'something' by **un dra bennak**.

109. 'Some' in the sense of 'a little' is expressed by **un nebeud**. Example: **un nebeud arc'hant** 'some money'. One also says **un tamm** lit. 'a bit, a morsel'.

Un nebeud also means 'some' in the sense of 'several': **un nebeud kêrioù** 'some towns'.

Finally, **un nebeud**, used by itself, means either 'a little' or 'some'.

110. 'Several' before a noun or a pronoun may also be expressed differently. One can use the expression **meur a**, always followed by the singular: **meur a zen** 'several people, many people'. The noun, this time in the plural, may be followed with **a zo** or **'zo**: **tud a zo**, **tud 'zo** 'several people, certain people'.

111. 'Some' used alone is rendered by **darn** or **lod**. Examples: **darn a lavar**, **lod a lavar** 'some say'.

112. Another way of expressing the idea of 'some, certain' is to use idioms like **den pe zen** 'one person or the other', lit. 'person or person'; **tra pe dra** 'one thing or the other'; **hini pe hini** 'one or the other'; **bro pe vro** 'one country or the other'.

Note: One can also say: *an den-mañ-den, an dra-mañ-dra,* etc.

ALL

113. 'All' in the sense of 'entirely' 'completely', is expressed with the aid of the word **holl**, placed generally after the word to which it relates: **ar bed-holl** 'the whole world'; **nec'het-holl** 'completely disturbed'; **rivinet-holl** 'completely ruined'.

Note I: 'Entirely' is also expressed, after a noun, by *a-bezh*; after an adjective or a verb by *krenn, a-grenn*. Examples: *an ti a-bezh* 'the whole of the house'; *diskaret krenn* 'completely demolished'; *adober a-grenn* 're-do completely'.

Note II: Besides *a-bezh*, there is the equivalent expression *en e bezh* 'in its totality' after a masculine singular noun; *en he fezh* after a feminine singular; *en o fezh* after a plural. Example: *ar vro en he fezh* 'the country in its entirety', *bro* 'country' being feminine.

114. 'All' meaning 'in totality', 'together', is expressed by **holl**, generally placed just before the word to which it relates: **an holl diez** 'all the houses'.

115. The pronoun 'all', is expressed by **an holl**.

116. 'All' in the sense of 'each', is expressed by **pep** followed by the singular: **pep ti** 'each house'.

It can also be expressed by **kement**, also followed by the singular. But in this case the noun is often accompanied by a proposition which completes it: **kement ti a welas** 'every house which he saw, each house he saw'.

Note I: 'Each' is expressed by *pep unan* or *pep hini*.
Note II: Note the expression *pep a* 'each his, each her'; *kanañ a rejont pep a ganaouenn* 'each one sang a song'; *roet e voe dezho pep a gontell* 'they were each given a knife'.

NONE

117. 'No, none' is expressed by **nep**, followed by the noun to which it relates: **nep ti** 'no house'.

The same idea is expressed more frequently with the aid of the adverb **ebet**, placed after the word to which it relates: **ti ebet** 'no house'.

118. 'Nothing' is expressed by **netra**, as well as by **tra**, **tra ebet**, and **netra ebet**.

119. 'No one' is expressed by **den**, **den ebet**, **nikun**, **hini**, **hini ebet**.

> *Note:* All these words, *nep*, *ebet*, etc., are used, as in French, with a verb in the negative: *ne gavis den* '*je ne trouvai personne*', 'I did not find anyone'.

OTHER

120. 'Other' is expressed by the aid of the word **all**, more rarely **arall**, which always follows the word it qualifies: **un ti all** 'another house'.

All is also a pronoun: **un all** 'another'.

> *Note I:* The word *ken*, placed before a noun, has the sense of 'other': *n'o doa ken youl nemet da ober vad* 'they had no other desire but to do good'.
> *Note II*: 'Other', meaning 'different' is expressed by *disheñvel*. Example: *disheñvel eo* 'it is different'.

121. 'Each other' is expressed by **an eil hag egile**, if either of the two elements in question is masculine; if both of the two elements in question are feminine, one says **an eil hag eben**.

'One another' (more than two) is expressed by **an eil re hag ar re all**.

> *Note I:* One may also say: *an eil pe egile* 'one or the other'; *an eil koulz hag eben* 'the one as well as the other', etc. Concerning 'oneself', see §162.
> *Note II:* 'one…, the other…' is said *an eil…, egile…*; as well as *unan…, egile…*; or even *unan…, un all…*. Example: *an eil a c'hoarzh, egile a leñv* 'one laughs, the other cries'.
> 'The ones…, the others…' is said *darn…, darn…*; or *lod…, lod…*; or even *darn…, ar re all…*; etc. Example: *darn a zo a-du, darn a zo enep* 'some are for, the others against'.

SAME

122. 'Same', when it indicates an idea of similarity, is expressed by **hevelep**, which precedes the word to which it relates: **an hevelep maouez** 'the same woman'.

Note that **hevelep** also means 'such': **un hevelep maouez** 'such a woman'.

123. 'Same', when it indicates an idea of exactness or precision, is expressed by **end-eeun**, which follows the word to which it relates: **ar vaouez end-eeun** 'the very woman'.

Used in isolation, it is expressed by **zoken**.

> *Note:* It is possible to say: *ar vaouez zoken* 'even the woman'.

124. For the expressions 'myself', 'yourself', etc., see §91.

SUCH

125. 'One such, such', as an adjective, is expressed with the aid of the word **seurt** 'sort, kind', in expressions constructed in different ways: **ur seurt den**, **un den seurt-se**, **un den ar seurt-se**, **un den eus ar seurt** 'such a person'.

'One such', 'such a one' as a pronoun, is expressed **unan bennak**.

See also §122.

ONE

126. English 'one' or French '*on*' have no equivalent in Breton, although **an den** 'the person' is sometimes used in this sense: **ne oar mui an den petra ober** 'one doesn't know what to do'.

One generally expresses it with one of the plural personal pronouns 'we, you, they', or better with the impersonal verb: **ne c'hoarzher ket** 'one does not laugh'.

THE NUMERALS

CARDINAL AND ORDINAL NUMERALS

127. The following table gives the list of the cardinal and ordinal numerals. These function as adjectives:

Cardinal numerals		*Ordinal numerals*	
1	**unan**	1[añ], 1[vet]	**kentañ, unanvet**
2	**daou, div**	2[l], 2[vet]	**eil, eilvet**
3	**tri, teir**	3[e], 3[vet]	**trede, trivet, teirvet**
4	**pevar, peder**	4[e], 4[vet]	**pevare, pevarvet, pedervet**
5	**pemp**	5[vet]	**pempet, pempvet**
6	**c'hwec'h**	6[vet]	**c'hwec'hvet**
7	**seizh**	7[vet]	**seizhvet**
8	**eizh**	8[vet]	**eizhvet**
9	**nav**	9[vet]	**navet**
10	**dek**	10[vet]	**dekvet**
11	**unnek**	11[vet]	**unnekvet**
12	**daouzek**	12[vet]	**daouzekvet**
13	**trizek**	13[vet]	**trizekvet**
14	**pevarzek**	14[vet]	**pevarzekvet**
15	**pemzek**	15[vet]	**pemzekvet**
16	**c'hwezek**	16[vet]	**c'hwezekvet**
17	**seitek**	17[vet]	**seitekvet**
18	**triwec'h (eitek)**	18[vet]	**triwec'hvet (eitekvet)**
19	**naontek**	19[vet]	**naontekvet**
20	**ugent**	20[vet]	**ugentvet**
21	**unan warn-ugent**	21[vet]	**unanvet warn-ugent**
22	**daou warn-ugent**	22[vet]	**eilvet warn-ugent**
30	**tregont**	30[vet]	**tregontvet**
31	**unan ha tregont**	31[vet]	**unanvet ha tregont**
40	**daou-ugent**	40[vet]	**daou-ugentvet**
50	**hanter-kant**	50[vet]	**hanter-kantvet**
60	**tri-ugent**	60[vet]	**tri-ugentvet**
70	**dek ha tri-ugent**	70[vet]	**dekvet ha tri-ugent**
71	**unnek ha tri-ugent**	71[vet]	**unnekvet ha tri-ugent**
72	**daouzek ha tri-ugent**	72[vet]	**daouzekvet ha tri-ugent**
80	**pevar-ugent**	80[vet]	**pevar-ugentvet**

90	**dek ha pevar-ugent**	90^{vet}	**dekvet ha pevar-ugent**
91	**unnek ha pevar-ugent**	91^{vet}	**unnekvet ha pevar-ugent**
92	**daouzek ha pever-ugent**	92^{vet}	**daouzekvet ha pevar-ugent**
100	**kant**	100^{vet}	**kantvet**
101	**unan ha kant**	101^{vet}	**unanvet ha kant**
110	**dek ha kant**	110^{vet}	**dekvet ha kant**
120	**c'hwec'h-ugent**	120^{vet}	**c'hwec'h-ugentvet**
140	**seizh-ugent**	140^{vet}	**seizh-ugentvet**
150	**kant hanter-kant**	150^{vet}	**kant hanter-kantvet**
160	**eizh-ugent**	160^{vet}	**eizh-ugentvet**
180	**nav-ugent**	180^{vet}	**nav-ugentvet**
200	**daou c'hant**	200^{vet}	**daou c'hantvet**
1 000	**mil**	1 000^{vet}	**milvet**
1 000 000	**ur milion**	1 000 000^{vet}	**milionvet**

128. After a number, the noun remains in the singular: **ugent aval** 'twenty apples', unless the number is followed by the preposition **a** 'of': **ugent a avaloù** 'twenty apples'.

129. Unan, an adjectival numeral, should not be confused with the indefinite article **un**, **ur**, **ul**. On this see §34.

130. The following adjectival numerals have different forms in the masculine and in the feminine.

'Two': masculine, **daou**; feminine, **div**.
'Three': masculine, **tri**; feminine, **teir**.
'Four': masculine, **pevar**; feminine, **peder**.

Examples: **daou baotr**, **div blac'h** 'two boys, two girls'; **tri mab**, **teir merc'h** 'three sons, three daughters'; **pevar mevel**, **peder matezh** 'four waiters, four waitresses'.

Note I: This distinction between masculine and feminine is also found in compounds such as *daou warn-ugent*, *div warn-ugent* 'twenty-two': *daou baotr warn-ugent*, *div blac'h warn-ugent*.

Note II: The ordinal numeric adjectives *eil, eilvet, trede, pevare* are used for both genders. *Trivet* and *pevarvet* are used for the masculine; *teirvet* and *pedervet* for the feminine. These words are not subject to mutation after the article: *an teirvet* 'the third'; *an trede merc'h* 'the third daughter'.

131. One says: **daou zen warn-ugent** 'twenty-two people', **tri den ha tregont** 'thirty-three people', **an eizhvet den ha tri-ugent** 'the hundred sixtieth people'. In other words, when a compound number contains **war** or **ha**, the noun is placed in front of these words.

Note: If one uses the preposition *a* after the number, one says: *daou warn-ugent a dud* 'twenty-two people'.

OTHER NUMERALS

132. The first fractional numerals are: **hanter** 'a half', **trederenn** 'a third', **palevarzh** 'a fourth'.
The others are formed on the ordinals by replacing the ending **-vet** with the ending **-vedenn**. Example: **pempvedenn** 'a fifth', from **pempvet** 'fifth'; **unanvedenn warn-ugent** 'a twenty-first', from **unanvet warn-ugent** 'twenty-first'.

Note I: These words are nouns and, except for *hanter* and *palevarzh*, are feminine.
Note II: *Hanter* also acts as an adjective or an adverb and precedes the word to which it relates: *un hanter aval* 'half an apple', *hanter varv* 'half-dead'. Beside *hanter*, there is a feminine noun *hanterenn* 'half'.

133. The multiplicative numbers are formed with the word **kement**: **daou gement** 'double', **tri c'hement** 'triple', **pevar c'hement** 'quadruple', etc.

Note I: If these are taken as nouns, one adds the ending *-ad*, and writes them as single words: *an daougementad, an tric'hementad* 'the double, the triple', etc.
Note II: The word *gwech* 'time' is commonly used: *seizh gwech brasoc'h* 'seven times as big, seven times bigger'.

134. Expressions such as 'two by two', 'three by three', or 'two at a time', 'three at a time', or 'in twos', 'in threes' are expressed, either by **daou-ha-daou** (feminine **div-ha-div**), **tri-ha-tri** (feminine **teir-ha-teir**), or by **a-zaouoù, a-drioù**, etc.; or even **bep a zaou, bep a dri**, etc.

135. Alternation is expressed by the word **pep** (almost always mutated to **bep**) and the numeric adjective, whether cardinal or ordinal: **bep daou zevezh**, **bep eil devezh** 'every two days'.

Note: One says: *a zaou da zaou* 'by twos', *a dri da dri* 'by threes', etc.

136. For expressions like 'we two', 'you three', 'they four', 'all four', etc., see §92.

137. An approximated number can be expressed with the aid of the word **bennak**: **un ugent bennak** 'about twenty'. See §106, Note I.

One can also add to the number the ending **-ad**: **un ugentad** 'about twenty, a score or so', **ur c'hantad** 'about a hundred'; to **mil**, one adds **-iad**: **ur miliad** 'about a thousand'.

Note I: In these derivatives, the final *-k* of *dek* 'ten' becomes *-g*: *un degad* 'about ten'; *a-zegoù* 'by tens'.

Note II: One can say: *a-ugentadoù* 'by twenties'; *a-gantadoù* 'by hundreds' *a-viliadoù* 'by thousands', etc.

THE VERB

CONJUGATION

138. Breton has only one verbal conjugation, on the model of the regular verb **skrivañ** 'write', reproduced below. On the pages following the conjugations of the only five verbs which are considered irregular is given: **bez'añ** 'be', **endevout** 'have', **gouzout** 'know', **mont** 'go', and **ober** 'do'.

In the paradigms which follow, the verbs are given in the following format:

> first person singular
> second person singular
> third person singular (feminine in parentheses)
> first person plural
> second person plural
> third person plural
> impersonal passive

Note: In §224 it is explained that the graph *-z'-* is used in this book to show the written *-z-* which is pronounced in Leon but unpronounced in other parts of Brittany. The verb *bez'añ* (p. 50) is perhaps the best example of how the orthography has taken account of the unpronounced *-z-*, as in *bo* compared with *bez'o*. Note that in the imperfect habitual of *bez'añ* the *-z-* is *always* pronounced.

REGULAR VERB: **skrivañ**

Verbal Noun	*Present*	*Imperfect*
skrivañ 'write'	**skrivan**	**skriven**
	skrivez	**skrives**
Present Participle	**skriv**	**skrive**
o skrivañ	**skrivomp**	**skrivemp**
'writing'	**skrivit**	**skrivec'h**
	skrivont	**skrivent**
Verbal Adjective	**skriver**	**skrived**
skrivet 'written'		

Past Definite	*Future*	*Present Conditional*
skrivis	**skrivin**	**skrivfen**
skrivjout	**skrivi**	**skrivfes**
skrivas	**skrivo**	**skrivfe**
skrivjomp	**skrivimp**	**skrivfemp**
skrivjoc'h	**skrivot**	**skrivfec'h**
skrivjont	**skrivint**	**skrivfent**
skrivjod	**skrivor**	**skrivfed**

Past Conditional	*Imperative*
skrivjen	—
skrivjes	**skriv**
skrivje	**skrivet**
skrivjemp	**skrivomp**
skrivjec'h	**skrivit**
skrivjent	**skrivent**
skrivjed	—

IRREGULAR VERB: bez'añ

Verbal Noun	Present	Imperfect
bez'añ 'be'	on	oan
	out	oas
Present Participle	zo, eo, eus	oa
o vez'añ 'being'	omp	oamp
é vout (Gwenedeg)	oc'h	oac'h
Verbal Adjective	int	oant
bet 'been'	oar, eur	oad

Past Definite	Future	Present Conditional
boen	bin, bez'in	befen
boes	bi, bez'i	befes
boe	bo, bez'o	befe
boemp	bimp, bez'imp	befemp
boec'h	biot, bez'ot	befec'h
boent	bint, bez'int	befent
boed	bior, bez'or	befed

Past Conditional	Imperative
bijen	—
bijes	bez'
bije	bez'et
bijemp	bez'omp
bijec'h	bez'it
bijent	bez'ent
bijed	—

HABITUAL FORMS

Present	Imperfect
bez'an	bezen, emeden
bez'ez	bezes, emedes
bez'	beze, emede
bez'omp	bezemp, emedemp
bez'it	bezec'h, emedec'h
bez'ont	bezent, emedent
bez'er	bezed, emeded

LOCATIVE FORMS

Present	Imperfect
emaon	(em)edon, -en
emaout	(em)edos, -es
emañ	(em)edo, -e
emaomp	(em)edomp, -emp
emaoc'h	(em)edoc'h, -ec'h
emaint	(em)edont, -ent
emeur	(em)edod, -ed

IRREGULAR VERB: **endevout**

Verbal Noun	*Present*	*Imperfect*
endevout *or* **kaout**	**am eus**	**am boa**
'have'	**ac'h eus**	**az' poa**
	en (he) deus	**en (he) doa**
Present Participle	**hon eus**	**hor boa**
o kaout 'having'	**hoc'h eus**	**ho poa**
	o deus	**o doa**

Past Definite	*Future*		*Present Conditional*
am boe	**am bo**	**am bez'o**	**am befe**
az' poe	**az' po**	**ho pez'o**	**az' pefe**
en (he) doe	**en (he) devo**	**en devez'o**	**en (he) defe**
hor boe	**hor bo**	**hor bez'o**	**hor befe**
ho poe	**ho po**	**ho pez'o**	**ho pefe**
o doe	**o devo**	**o devez'o**	**o defe**

Past Conditional	*Imperative*	
am bije	**am bez'et**	**am bez'et**
az' pije	**az' pez'**	**az' pez'et**
en (he) dije	**en (he) defet**	**en (he) devez'et**
hor bije	**hor bez'et**	**hor bez'et**
ho pije	**ho pet**	**ho pez'et**
o dije	**o defent**	**o devez'et**

HABITUAL FORMS

Present	*Imperfect*
am bez'	**am beze**
az' pez'	**az' peze**
en (he) devez'	**an (he) deveze**
hor bez'	**hor beze**
ho pez'	**ho peze**
o devez'	**o deveze**

IRREGULAR VERB: gouzout

Verbal Noun	Present	Imperfect
gouzout 'know'	**gouzon**	**gouien**
	gouzout	**gouies**
Present Participle	**goar**	**gouie**
o c'houzout	**gouzomp**	**gouiemp**
'knowing'	**gouzoc'h**	**gouiec'h**
Verbal Adjective	**gouzont**	**gouient**
gouezet 'known'	**gouzer**	**gouied**

Past Definite	Future	Present Conditional
gouezis	**gouezin**	**goufen**
gouejout	**gouezi**	**goufes**
gouezas	**gouezo**	**goufe**
gouejomp	**gouezimp**	**goufemp**
gouejoc'h	**gouezot**	**goufec'h**
gouejont	**gouezint**	**goufent**
gouejod	**gouezor**	**goufed**

Past Conditional	Imperative
gouijen	—
gouijes	**gouez**
gouije	**gouezet**
gouijemp	**gouezomp**
gouijec'h	**gouezit**
gouijent	**gouezent**
gouijed	—

Note: Gouzout is the most irregular of Breton verbs; it is commonly conjugated on one of a number of variant roots: *gouiañ/gouiet, goarout,* and *gouvez'out.*

IRREGULAR VERB: **mont**

Verbal Noun	*Present*	*Imperfect*
mont 'go'	**an**	**aen**
	ez	**aes**
Present Participle	**a, ya**	**ae, yae**
o vont 'going'	**eomp**	**aemp**
	it	**aec'h**
Verbal Adjective	**eont**	**aent**
aet 'gone'	**eer**	**aed**

Past Definite	*Future*	*Present Conditional*
is	**in**	**afen**
ejout	**i**	**afes**
eas, yeas	**ay, aio, yelo**	**afe, yafe**
ejomp	**aimp**	**afemp**
ejoc'h	**eot**	**afec'h**
ejont	**aint**	**afent**
ejod	**eor**	**afed**

Past Conditional	*Imperative*
ajen	—
ajes	**a, kae**
aje, yaje	**aet**
ajemp	**eomp, deomp**
ajec'h	**it, kit**
ajent	**aent**
ajed	—

IRREGULAR VERB: ober

Verbal Noun	Present	Imperfect
ober 'do'	**gran**	**graen**
	grez	**graes**
Present Participle	**gra**	**grae**
oc'h ober 'doing'	**greomp**	**graemp**
Verbal Adjective	**grit**	**graec'h**
graet 'done'	**greont**	**graent**
	greer	**graed**

Past Definite	Future	Present Conditional
gris	**grin**	**grafen**
grejout	**gri**	**grafes**
greas, geure	**gray, graio**	**grafe**
grejomp	**graimp**	**grafemp**
grejoc'h	**greot**	**grafec'h**
grejont	**graint**	**grafent**
grejod	**greor**	**grafed**

Past Conditional	Imperative
grajen	—
grajes	**gra**
graje	**graet**
grajemp	**greomp**
grajec'h	**grit**
grajent	**graent**
grajed	—

THE VERBAL NOUN

139. The verbal noun is formed, either from the root itself, like **lenn** 'read', or from the root and an ending: **-añ**, **-iñ**, **-at**, **-out**, **-al**, **-n**, -**ezh**, **-er**, **-en**.

Examples: **hadañ** 'sow', **debriñ** 'eat', **lakaat** 'put', **kavout** 'find', **nijal** 'fly', **eren** 'tie', **laerezh** 'steal, rob', **embreger** 'undertake', **dougen** 'carry, wear'.

Note I: Some verbs have several forms of the verbal noun: *aotreañ*, *aotren* 'permit'.

Note II: From region to region one can find that the verbal noun endings are almost interchangeable. In Leon, *-añ* is common; in Gwened, it doesn't exist at all.

140. In certain verbal nouns, the vowel of the root is altered. These are especially the verbal nouns in **-eiñ, -el, -iñ**.

Examples: **skeiñ** 'strike' root **sko**; **gervel** 'call', root **galv**; **terriñ** 'break', root **torr**.

The verb **dont** 'come' is conjugated on the root **deu**. Its participle is **deuet** or **deut**. In the imperative, the second person singular is **deus** 'come!', the second person plural **deuit** or **deut** 'come!'.

141. The verbal noun is sometimes used as an ordinary noun. It is then treated like a masculine singular: **an debriñ hag an evañ** 'the food and the drink'; **ober un aozañ** 'make a reparation' lit. 'make a repair'.

THE PRESENT PARTICIPLE

142. The present participle is formed with the aid of the particle **o** (**oc'h** before a vowel, **ouzh** before a personal pronoun): **o tebriñ** 'eating', **oc'h evañ** 'drinking', **ouzh e welout** 'seeing him'. The forms **é** and **ec'h** are used in Gwenedeg.

143. According to the sense, **o** can be replaced by **en ur**, **a-greiz**, **dre**, etc.: **en ur gerzhout** 'while marching'; **a-greiz komz** 'while speaking'; **dre labourat** 'by (dint of) working'.

THE COMPOUND TENSES AND AUXILIARIES

144. Endevout 'have' and **bez'añ** 'be' are used as auxiliaries in the same conditions as in English and French to form the compound tenses: perfect (indefinite past), pluperfect, past perfect, future perfect, present conditiona, past conditional. (English doesn't make some of these verbal distinctions in translation.)

Here are examples with the verb **kavout** 'find' and the auxiliary **endevout**:

Perfect:	**kavet en deus**	'he has found'
Pluperfect:	**kavet en doa**	'he had found'
Past Perfect:	**kavet en doe**	'he had found'
Future Perfect:	**kavet en devo**	'he will have found'
Pres. Conditional:	**kavet en defe**	'he would have found'
Past Conditional:	**kavet en dije**	'he would have found'

Here are examples with the verb **kouezhañ** 'fall' and the auxiliary **bez'añ**:

Perfect:	**kouezhet eo**	'he has fallen'
Pluperfect:	**kouezhet e oa**	'he had fallen'
Past Perfect:	**kouezhet e voe**	'he had fallen'
Future Perfect:	**kouezhet e vo**	'he will have fallen'
Pres. Conditional:	**kouezhet e vefe**	'he would have fallen'
Past Conditional:	**kouezhet e vije**	'he would have fallen'

For the use of **endevout** with transitive and **bez'añ** with intransitive verbs, compare the French *il a trouvé* 'he has found' and *il est tombé* 'he has fallen'. Intransitive verbs, such as verbs of motion, take **bez'añ** as the auxiliary.

Note I: The auxiliary can precede the verb: *eñ en deus kavet* 'he has found'; *eñ a zo kouezhet* 'he has fallen'.

Note II: The verbal noun of the verb 'have' is generally *kaout*: one says *mat eo kaout fiziañs* 'it is good to have faith'; one says less often *mat eo endevout* (or *en devout*) *fiziañs*. Note that the verbal noun of *endevout* varies according to the person: *am bout, az' pout, en devout, he devout, hor bout, ho pout, o devout*; Examples: *kavet em eus hep am bout klasket* 'I have

48

found without having looked'; *c'hwi a zlefe ho pout mezh* 'you should be
ashamed' lit. 'you should have shame'.

Note III: The locative forms of *bez'añ* in the present (*emaon, emaout,*
etc.) are never used to form the compound tenses.

145. In the past infinitive, **endevout** is often replaced by **bez'añ**.
Example: **bez'añ hadet** 'have sown'.

146. Ober 'do' serves frequently as an auxiliary, especially when the
verb is to be stressed. It takes the verbal noun: **skrivañ a ra** 'he writes',
lit. 'writing he does'.

Note I: The normal unmarked declarative sentence in the north of
Brittany is formed with *ober: debriñ a ran* 'I am eating'. The same is
formed with the subject expressed in southern Brittany: *me a zebr.* To
stress the agent, one can say: *me eo a zo o tebriñ 'I'm* eating'; to stress the
action, one can say: *o tebriñ emaon 'I'm eating'.*

Note II: The verb *gouzout* 'know' does not always take *ober,* but also
itself: *gouzout a ra* 'he knows' or *gouzout a oar.*

147. Likewise, when one wishes to stress the verb, a special form is used
in which the phrase begins with the auxiliary **bez'añ**, usually shortened
to **bez'** (with a real orthographic apostrophe), after which the verb follows
in the desired tense: **bez' e hadas** 'he sowed'.

THE HABITUAL TENSES

148. In the present and imperfect, **bez'añ** and **endevout** have forms
expressing habitualness, long duration or the frequent repetition of an
action: **klañv e vez' bep sizhun** 'he is sick every week'; **poan hor bez'
o labourat e-pad ar goañv** 'we find it hard to work in winter'.

THE LOCATIVE TENSES

149. Bez'añ also has special present and imperfect forms, which
express location or momentary situation: **emañ e Brest** 'he is in Brest';
edo o vervel 'he was dying'.

THE CONDITIONAL

150. The conditional is used whenever there is an idea of doubt, in particular after the conjunctions **ma** or **pa** in the sense of 'if': **ma teufe e vefen laouen** 'if he came I would be happy'; **pa vefen klañv ne zeufen ket** 'if I were sick I wouldn't come'.

Note I: After *mar* 'if', the indicative is used: *mar fell deoc'h ez' in* 'if you wish I will go'. See §196.

Note II: There is a present conditional in *-f-* and a past conditional in *-j-*: *deufe, deuje* 'he would come'. In current usage these are confused, being used one for the other without distinction. Nevertheless, the learner is counselled to observe the agreement of tense: *me a gred e teufe* 'I believe that he would come'; *me a grede e teuje* 'I believed that he would have come'.

THE SUBJUNCTIVE

151. Breton has no subjunctive per se. To translate the French subjunctive one uses either the future indicative, or the conditional.

Regarding a command or a wish, with an idea of futurity, one generally uses the future: **fellout a ra din ma teuio** 'I want him to come' (*je veux qu'il vienne*); **gant ma teuio** 'would that he came' (*pourvu qu'il vienne*).

In other cases one generally uses the conditional: **aon en deus na zeufe ket** 'he fears he may not come' (*il craint qu'il ne vienne pas*).

Note: The French subjunctive, when it is equivalent to the imperative, is expressed by the imperative in Breton, or by the optative (see §170). Example: *deuent* ou *ra zeuint* 'let them come' (*qu'ils viennent*).

REMARKS ON THE IRREGULAR VERBS

152. The compound tenses of **endevout** 'have' are formed with the aid of **bet**, the past participle of **bez'añ**. Example: **me am eus bet** 'I have had'. **Bez'añ** serves as its own auxiliary: **me a zo bet** 'I have been'.

153. In the first and second persons singular of **endevout**, one sometimes finds **em, ec'h, ez'** instead of **am, ac'h, az'**. Examples: **bet em eus** 'I have had'; **n'ec'h eus ket bet** 'you haven't had'; **atav ez' po va skoazell** 'you will always have my help'.

This happens when, as the usual rule requires, either the verbal particle **e**, or the negative particle **ne** precedes the verb (see §§166 and 171). **Ne'm** and **ne'c'h** are found, but **n'em** and **n'ec'h** should be preferred as written forms.

154. In the third person singular of the present, there are three forms of **bez'añ**: **zo**, **eo**, **eus**, not counting the habitual and locative forms.

Zo is used in the affirmative, when the subject precedes the verb: **me a zo** 'I am'.

Eo is used in other cases: **brav eo** 'it's nice'.

Eus means 'there is, there are': **eno ez' eus tud** 'there are people there'.

> *Note*: 'There is' (French *il y a*) is expressed by *a zo* or *'zo* if one begins the sentence with the object noun of 'there is': *tud a zo* or *tud 'zo* 'there are people'. Likewise in temporal expressions, where French *il y a* corresponds to English *ago*: *pell 'zo* 'long ago'. In the negative one always says *eus*: *n'eus ket a dud* 'there are no people'; *n'eus ket pell* 'not long ago'.
>
> In the other tenses the appropriate form of the verb 'be' is used: *tud a oa* 'there were people'; *tud a vo* 'there will be people'.
>
> One may also begin the sentence by saying: *bez' ez' eus* 'there is, there are', *bez' e oa* 'there was, there were', etc.; *bez' ez' eus bara* 'there is bread'. In southern Brittany where *bout* is used instead of *bez'añ*, *bout eus* and *bout 'zo* are used.

155. In the third person singular, in most of the tenses, one finds two forms of **mont** 'go': **a**, **ya**; or three: **ay**, **aio**, **yelo**. The form which begins with **y-** is only used in the affirmative, when the subject precedes the verb: **me a ya** 'we will go'.

> *Note*: One can think of this *y-* as an unusual form of the verbal particle. The verbal particle has forms in some dialects where the linking consonant differs; one can consider the *-y-* in the same light: *bremañ ez an da zebriñ* 'now I go to eat' can have *eh an* or *e yan* (**ey an*) instead of *ez'*.

156. After the verbal particles **a**, **e**, the negative particles **ne**, **na**, and the conjunctions **ma**, **pa**, the **g-** is lost in the forms of **gouzout** 'know' and of **ober** 'do' which begin with this consonant: **hi a oar** 'she knows'; **ne ra ket** 'he doesn't do'.

THE PASSIVE

157. There are in the simple tenses special forms for the impersonal passive: **un den a weler** 'a person is seen'; **n'em anavezed ket** 'one didn't know me, no one knew me'. See §126.

THE IMPERSONAL

158. In the impersonal, the subject is not expressed: **glav a ra** 'it's raining', lit. 'rain does'; **noziñ a ra** 'night is falling'.

Note I: The feminine sometimes makes its appearance in phrases of this kind. Thus one can find: *brav e oa anezhi* 'it was nice', lit. 'nice was by her'.

Note II: A number of verbs which are impersonal in French correspond in Breton, as in English, to verbs which take prepositions: *kavout a ra din* 'it seems to me', lit. 'finding does to me'; *fellout a ra din* 'I must', lit. 'lacking does to me'; *bernout a ra din* 'it's important to me', lit. 'mattering does to me'. The corresponding French impersonals are: *il me semble, il me faut, il m'importe*.

One can also say: *krediñ a ra din* 'I believe'; *soñjal a ra din* 'I think'.

In the negative, one says: *ne gav ket din* 'it doesn't seem to me', *ne fell ket din* 'I don't want to', etc.

ANOMALIES

159. Verbs like **glebiañ** 'soak', ending in **-añ**, in which **-i-** is consonantal [j], do not retain this **-i-** except before **-a**, **-e**, **-o**: one writes **glebias, glebie, glebio**, etc., but **gleb, glebis, glebjomp, glebfe**, etc.

If these verbs end in **-niañ**, like **leuniañ** 'fill', or in **-liañ**, like **heuliañ** 'follow', the **-n-** and the **-l-** become **-gn-** and **-(i)lh-** whenever the **-i-** disappears: **leugn, leugnis, leugnjomp, heuilhin, heuilhfe**, etc.

160. Verbs whose root is in **-a-**, like **pesketa** 'fish', **brasaat** 'enlarge', in **-eu-**, like **dont** 'come', or in **-o-**, like **reiñ** 'give', take in the third person singular future the ending **-io** or **-y**: **pesketaio, pesketay**; **brasaio, brasay**; **deuio, deuy**; **roio, roy**. For more, on the subject of **dont**, see §140.

161. The root of certain verbs sometimes changes under the influence of an ending. In this case, both regular and irregular forms coexist: **lavarout** 'say' gives **lavarit** and **livirit**, **lavarot** and **leverot**; **karout** 'love' gives **karit** and **kirit**, **karot** and **kerot**. **Gallout** 'be able' is conjugated on two roots, **gall** and **gell**, etc.

THE REFLEXIVE VERB

162. To form the reflexive verb, **en em** is placed before the verb in every tense and in every person: **en em veuliñ** 'praise oneself'; **al laer a zo en em lazhet** 'the thief has killed himself'; **en em welout a rit en dour** 'you see yourself in the water'.

This same **en em** also serves to form the reciprocal verb: **n'en em garont ket kenetrezo** 'they do not love one another'; **arabat en em gannañ** 'it is forbidden to fight one another'.

THE VERB AND ITS SUBJECT

163. The personal pronoun is not generally expressed (see §64). Example: **ma hadan** 'if I sow'; **ne hadas ket** 'he did not sow'.

164. When the subject is expressed, the verb is put into the third person singular, whether the subject be a pronoun or a plural noun: **me a had** 'I am sowing'; **e vreudeur a hadas** 'his brothers sowed'.

165. In the negative, however, the verb agrees with its subject, if the subject precedes it: **me ne hadan ket** 'I am not sowing'; **e vreudeur ne hadjont ket** 'his brothers didn't sow'. But the third person singular is used if the subject follows the verb: **n'emañ ket va c'hoarezed e kêr** 'my sisters are not at home'.

THE VERBAL PARTICLES

166. The verb is generally preceded by a particle, except as a verbal noun and in the imperative. This particle is **a** if the verb is preceded by its subject or a direct object: **me a had** 'I am sowing'; **tud a welan** 'I see people'; **skeiñ a rankas** 'he had to strike'.

This particle is **e** (**ez'** or **ec'h** before a vowel) if the verb is preceded by an indirect object or by an adverb: **eviti e laboure** 'he was working for her'; **neuze ez' eas kuit** 'then he left'.

Note I: The rule for particles after *bez'añ* is this: *a* comes after the subject, *e* after the attribute or object: *me a oa* 'I was', *klañv e oa* 'he was ill'; *eno e oa trouz* 'there was noise there'.

Note II: After conjunctions other than *ma, mar, pa* (for which see §167), the particle *e* is used: *koulskoude e felle dezhañ mont kuit* 'nevertheless he wanted to leave'; *ne gomzo ket, pe e vezo tamallet* 'he won't speak, or he will be blamed'; *hag e labour atav* 'and he always works'.

There is however one case in which the conjunctions *pe* and *hag* are followed by *a*: when they connect two verbs preceded by a subject or a direct object: *ar re-se a blego pe a varvo* 'those people will submit or they will die'; *ar plac'h a gomze hag a gane* 'the girl spoke and sang'; *da gerent a gari hag a zouji* 'you will love and respect your parents'.

167. The particle is omitted when the verb is preceded by **ma**, **mar**, **pa**, **ne**, **na**, **en em**, or by a personal pronoun: **kozh e oa pa varvas** 'he was old when he died'; **warc'hoazh he gwelin** 'tomorrow I will see her'. The pronouns **'m** and **'z** are exceptional; see §153.

Note I: The particle is omitted after two rarely used conjunctions, *aba* 'since' and *endra* 'while': *aba veve* 'since he lived'; *endra gomze* 'while he spoke'.

Note II: Before the forms of the verbs *bez'añ* 'be' and *mont* 'go' which begin with vowels, *ma'z* and *pa'z* are used instead of *ma* and *pa*: *ma'z afen di* 'if I went there'; *pa'z on bet eno* 'when I was there'. The forms of *bez'añ* in the imperfect (*oan, oas,* etc.) often make an exception to this rule: *pa oan* 'if I was'.

168. The particle is sometimes omitted before certain verbs, in particular **bez'añ**. Note that the locative forms of **bez'añ** (**emaon**, **emaout**, etc.) never take the particle.

The particle is omitted before every form of **endevout**.

169. Before some verbs, the particle **e** can begin a sentence: **ez' an da lavarout** 'I am going to say'; **e c'hallfe bez'añ ma...** 'it could be that...'; **e kredan aes ez...** 'I believe easily that...'.

170. There is an optative particle **ra**, which is placed before the verb in the future to express a wish: **ra zeuio buan en-dro** 'may he return quickly, I hope he returns quickly'.

Note: The optative is also formed with the aid of the verbal noun and the preposition *da*: *dezhañ da zont en-dro buan* lit. 'to him to come back quickly'.

NEGATION

171. Negation is expressed with the aid of the words **ne ... ket** (French *ne ... pas*) surrounding the verb: **ne skrivan ket** 'I do not write'.

In compound tenses the words **ne ... ket** surround the auxiliary: **ne voe ket lazhet** 'he was not killed'.

172. Ne is replaced by **na** in the imperative: **na ganit ket** 'do not sing'.

Na is used also to express 'that not, which not' completing or determining a noun: **un dra na c'houlennen ket** 'a thing which I did not ask'. See §204.

Finally, **na** is used in place of **ne** after **ken** 'until', **evit** 'for' and expressions indicating a fear, like **gant aon** 'for fear of', **evit mirout** 'to prevent'. Examples: **gortozit ken na skrivo** 'wait until he writes'; **en em guzhit evit na welo ket ac'hanoc'h** 'hide yourself so he won't see you'; **mont a ran kuit gant aon na zeufent** 'I am leaving for fear that they would come'; **hastit, evit mirout na vefe re ziwezhat** 'hurry, to prevent his (her, its) being too late'.

173. In the infinitive, there is no negative form, because negative particles precede the verb and the infinitive is a (verbal) *noun*. Negation is supplied by means of expressions like: **chom hep** lit. 'rest without'; **tremen hep** lit. 'pass without'; **mirout a** 'keep from'. Examples: **chom hep fiñval** 'not move'; **tremen hep debriñ** 'not eat'; **mirout a redek** 'not run'. But it is possible to find **na** before a verbal noun: **na grediñ** or **na grediñ ket** 'not believe'.

174. Ket is generally omitted when another word of the sentence implies a negation: **ne c'hoarzh ken** 'he (she) laughs no more'; **n'o gwelan mui** 'I see them no more'; **n'o c'haras morse** 'he never loved them'; **n'eus den ebet aze** 'there is no one there'.

Ket is also omitted in sentences like those given as examples in §172: **gortozit ken na skrivo**, etc.

175. Ne and **na** are often elided before a vowel, though there is no absolute rule for this: **n'anaveze netra** or **ne anaveze netra** 'he didn't know anything'. The elision always takes place before a personal pronoun:

n'o anaveze ket 'he didn't know them'. See §56 for the particular case of the first and second persons singular.

176. Before the forms of the verbs **bez'añ** and **mont** which begin with a vowel, **ne** and **na** may take a **d-** prefixed to the verb: **ne don ket** 'I am not'; **ne deas ket** 'he didn't go'.

Note: This also occurs after the conjunction *mar* 'if': *mar don* 'if I am'; *mar deas* 'if he went'.

THE ADVERB

177. Breton has temporal adverbs, locative adverbs, quantitative adverbs, etc.: **atav** 'always', **eno** 'there', **kalz** 'much', etc.

178. One can form an adverb of manner from an adjective by placing the particle **ez'** before it. Example: **leal** 'loyal', **ez' leal** 'loyally'.

179. The adverb of manner is usually confused with the adjective: **derc'hel a ra leal d'e c'her** 'he keeps his word loyally'; **souezhet-bras eo bet** 'he was greatly astonished'; **ne fiñvas ket an disterañ** 'he did not move in the slightest'.

180. The adverb related to an adjective or to a past participle is generally connected to it by a hyphen: **klañv-fall** 'gravely ill'; **souezhet-meurbet** 'very astonished'; **paour a-walc'h** 'poor enough'.

181. The noun can act as an adverb after an adjective: **gwenn-erc'h** 'white as snow'; **sec'h-korn** 'dry as a horn'.

THE PREPOSITION

182. The most common prepositions combine with the personal pronoun: **evit** 'for', **evito** 'for them'. In effect, the prepositions are conjugated. The tables on the following pages give the forms of the various prepositions in these pronominal conjugations.

Note: On Table B following will be found the word *eme*, which is not a preposition, but a verb meaning 'says' and 'said'. This word conjugates as though it were a preposition, rather than a verb: *emez'on* 'I said', *emez'out* 'you said', etc. With the first person singular pronoun, it sometimes forms a combined form *emeve* 'I said', instead of *emez'on*. Likewise, *eget* 'than', a conjunction, and *estreget* 'other than' is a sort of adjective combined with *eget*.

183. The prepositions which do not appear in the table can be classed in three categories: those which combine with the personal pronoun with the aid of another conjugated preposition, those which conjugate in decomposition, and those which do not conjugate.

184. Among the most usual prepositions in the first category, prepositions which combine with the personal pronoun with the aid of another conjugated prepositions, are: **a-dreñv**, **a-drek** 'behind', **a-dreuz** 'through', **dreist** 'over', **enep**, **a-enep** 'against', **e-tal** 'near to'; these combine with the pronoun with the aid of the preposition **da**: **a-dreñv din** 'behind me', **dreist dezhañ** 'over him', **a-enep dezhi** 'against her', **e-tal dimp** 'near us', etc.

The prepositions **betek** 'up to' and **etrezek** 'toward' combine with the preposition **e** 'in': **betek ennon** 'up to me', **etrezek ennañ** 'toward him'.

185. In the second category, prepositions which conjugate in decomposition, are those prepositions beginning in **e**: **e-kichen** 'near', **e-keñver** 'towards', **e-kreiz** 'in the middle of', **e-lec'h** 'in the place of', **e-mesk** 'among', **e-touez** 'among', etc. They decompose and the possessive adjective is placed between the **e** and the rest of the preposition: **em c'hichen** 'near me', **ez' keñver** 'towards you', **en e greiz** 'in the middle of it', **en he lec'h** 'in her place', **en hor mesk** 'among us', **en ho touez** 'among you', etc.

Likewise, prepositions beginning in **diwar-**: **diwar-benn** 'concerning' gives **diwar ho penn** 'about you'.

Then there are prepositions beginning in **war-**: **war-dro** 'about', **war-lerc'h** 'after'. They decompose in the same fashion: **war va zro** 'about me', **war o lerc'h** 'after them'. Note the expression **ober war va zro** 'to look after me'.

The case of other prepositions is a bit more complicated: **a-zivout** 'about, concerning' gives **war va divout** 'concerning me'; **a-raok** 'before' gives **em raok** 'before me'; **a-berzh** 'on behalf of' gives **eus va ferzh** 'on my behalf', **eus hor perzh** 'from us' lit. 'from our part'.

Note: Goude 'after' is sometimes formed thus: *em goude* 'after me', *ez' koude* 'after you', *en e c'houde* 'after him', etc.

186. In the third category, those prepositions with are not conjugated, appear, among prepositions currently in use: **a-hed** 'the length of', **adal**, **adalek** 'since', **e-barzh** 'inside', **e-pad** 'during', **e-giz** 'like', **eus** 'from', **ouzhpenn** 'in addition to'.

Note I: Since not all of these prepositions are conjugated, they are replaced by prepositions having the same meaning, and which themselves are conjugated. Thus *eus* 'from' is replaced by *a*, which means the same. Thus one says *ac'hanon* 'from me', *ouzhpenn din* 'in addition to me', *ennon* 'inside me', *ouzh va hed* 'the length of me'. It is possible to conjugate *e-giz* with *egiston*, or to say *e-giz din*.

Note II: In the tables following, this edition follows the presentation given in Kervella 1976.

TABLE OF PREPOSITIONS
I. Endings in *-on*
A. Without linking consonants

Stem + endings	Stem **-t** > **-d-** in 1,2 + endings
dindanon	**davedon**
dindanout	**davedout**
dindanañ	**davetañ**
dindani	**daveti**
dindanomp	**davedomp**
dindanoc'h	**davedoc'h**
dindano/dindane	**daveto/davete**

    dindan 'under'   *davet* 'towards, to'
    dreist 'over'   *eget* 'than'
    hervez' 'according to'   *estreget* 'other than'
                            evit 'for, in order to'
                            nemet 'but, except'
                            panevet 'if it were not for'

B. With linking **-n-**

Stem in **-n** + **-n-** + endings	Stem in **-r** + **-n-** + endings
ennon	**warnon**
ennout	**warnout**
ennañ	**warn(ezh)añ**
enni	**warn(ezh)i**
ennomp	**warnomp**
ennoc'h	**warnoc'h**
enno/enne	**warn(ezh)o/warn(ezh)e**

    en 'in, into'   *war* 'on'
                            diwar 'from, because of'

C. With linking **-t-**

Stem + **-t-** + endings	Stem + **-t-** (**-d-** in 1,2) + endings
egiston	**eveldon**
egistout	**eveldout**
egistañ	**eveltañ**
egisti	**evelti**
egistomp	**eveldomp**
egistoc'h	**eveldoc'h**
egisto/egiste	**evelto/evelte**

    a-zioc'h 'above'   *evel* 'like'
    e-giz 'like'   *hep* 'without'

D. With linking -z-

Stem in -**e** + -**z**- + endings	Stem in -**k** > -**z**- + endings
drezon	**a-raozon**
drezout	**a-raozout**
drezañ	**a-raozañ**
drezi	**a-raozi**
drezomp	**a-raozomp**
drezoc'h	**a-raozoc'h**
drezo/dreze	**a-raozo/a-raoze**
dre 'through, by means of'	*a-raok* 'before'
eme 'said, says' (verb)	*dirak* 'in front of, before'
etre 'between'	*rak* 'in front of, against'

E. Irregular	II. Endings in -*in*
	A. With 3 in -**ezh**
Stem + -**ezh**- in 3 + endings	Stem + -**ezh**- in 3 + endings
ac'hanon	**din**
ac'hanout	**dit**
anezhañ	**dezhañ**
anezhi	**dezhi**
ac'hanomp	**dimp, deomp**
ac'hanoc'h	**deoc'h**
anezho/anezhe	**dezho/dezhe**
a (eus) 'from, of'	*da* 'at, to, for'

B. With stem in -**nt**	C. With stem in -**zh**
Stem -**nt** > -**n**- in 1,2 + endings	Stem -**zh** > -**t**- in 3 + endings
ganin	**ouzhin**
ganit	**ouzhit**
gantañ	**outañ**
ganti	**outi**
ganimp, **ganeomp**	**ouzhimp**
ganeoc'h	**ouzhoc'h**
ganto/gante	**outo/oute**
gant 'with'	*ouzh* 'at, beside, against'
digant 'from'	*diouzh* 'from, according to'

Note: Examination of the tables will show that there are two main ending classes:

I   *-on, -out, -añ, -i; -omp, -oc'h, -o* (or *-e*)
II   *-in, -it, -añ, -i; -imp, -eoc'h, -o* (or *-e*)

These vary rather widely from dialect to dialect as to which endings are used with which prepositional stems. Some dialects only use one class exclusively, while others mix them in various ways. This book gives the Unified Breton written standard—but the learner will hear many variations.

187. There are in Breton many prepositions composed of several elements or prepositional locutions. They generally end in a simple preposition (almost always **da**), and conjugating them offers therefore no difficulty.

Some are listed here: **abalamour da**, **en abeg da**, **en askont da** 'because of', **en arbenn da** 'towards', **en-dro da** 'around', **hep gouzout da N.** 'unknown to N.', **a-dal da** 'facing, in front of', **pell diouzh** 'far from', **a-us da** 'above'.

THE CONJUNCTION

188. The principal conjunctions are: **ha** 'and', which becomes **hag** before a vowel: **pe** 'or'; **na** 'nor', which becomes **nag** before a vowel; **hogen, met** 'but'; **rak** 'for, because'; **peogwir** 'because', **ma** 'that, if'; **mar** 'if'; **pa** 'if, when, because'.

189. A conjunction is generally connected to the verb which follows by the verbal particle **e**. Example: **hag e kouezhas** 'and he fell'; **peogwir e varvas** 'because he died'. See §166.

190. Hogen, met, rak may not be followed by a verb. One says **rak e vamm a varvas** 'for his mother died', and not *rak e varvas e vamm.

191. After the conjunctions **ma, mar, pa**, the conjunction **e** is not used. See §167.

Note: The conjunctions *ma* and *pa* become *m'* and *p'* before a personal pronoun: *p'ho kwelas* 'when he saw you'. But in the first and second persons singular, *ma'm, pa'm, ma'z', pa'z'* are used.

This also sometimes happens before the forms of the verb *bez'añ* 'be' and of the verb *endevout* 'have': *m'eo bet* 'if he has been'; *p'o deus lavaret* 'when they have said'. This completes Note II of §167.

192. Beside the conjunctions per se there exist, as in French, a certain number of conjunctive locutions. Many of these end in **ma**. Example: **o vez'añ ma** 'given that'; **a-raok ma** 'before that'; **goude ma** 'after that'; **e-pad ma, e-keit ha ma** 'during that'; **a-feur ma** 'according as', etc.

Some others end in **na**. Examples: **gant aon na** 'for fear that'; **ken na** 'until that'.

Note: Do not confuse this *na*, the negative particle discussed in §172, with the conjunction *na* discussed in §188, which means 'neither'. They are two distinct words. *Na* 'neither' does not cause mutation; *na* 'not' causes the soft mutation.

193. When a conjunctive locution is composed of a preposition and of **ma**, the **ma** can be replaced by **da**, in order to conjugate **da**; the verb then follows as a verbal noun. Example: instead of **a-raok ma varvas**

'before he died', one may say **a-raok dezhañ mervel** lit. 'before to him dying'.

Sometimes the preposition of the conjunctive locution is itself the conjugated preposition. Example: **evit ma kano** 'in order that he sings', or **evit dezhañ kanañ** lit. 'for to him singing', or **evitañ da ganañ** 'for him to sing'.

194. Note in particular the way in which the conjunction 'that' is expressed in Breton in isolation (that is, outside of any conjunctive locution). It is generally expressed by the conjunction **ma** or by the verbal particle **e**.

E is mostly used with verbs expressing an opinion, a belief, a state of existing things, like **krediñ** 'believe', **soñjal** 'think', **gouzout** 'know', **merzout** 'observe, notice', **lavarout** 'say'.

Example: **krediñ a ran e teuio** 'I believe that he will come'.

Ma is mostly used after verbs expressing a command, a wish, a desire, a state of things one would like to realize, like **gourc'hemenn** 'order', **karout** 'love, want', **c'hoantaat** 'desire'.

Example: **gourc'hemenn a ran ma teuio** 'I order him to come'.

But this distinction is not absolute.

195. When the verb is in the negative, **ne** and **na**, the negative particles, replace **e** and **ma**. Examples: **ha ne gouezhas ket** 'and he did not fall'; **peogwir ne varvas ket** 'because he did not die'; **o vezañ na wele ket** 'given that he did not see'.

Note: But sometimes *ma* is left before *ne*. Example: *o vezañ ma ne wele ket.*

196. The conjunction 'if' is generally expressed by **ma**, **mar**, or **pa**. Examples: **laouen e vefen ma teufe** 'I would be happy if he came'; **mar** is not regularly used except before the indicative: **laouen e vin mar deu** 'I will be happy if he comes'; this is only true in the affirmative; in the negative **ma** is used: **ma ne skriv ket din, ez' in d'e welout** 'if he doesn't write to me, I will go to see him'.

However, when 'if' means 'whether', as in the phrases 'ask if, not know if', **ha** must be used. Examples: **goulenn a reas ha dont a raje** 'he asked whether he would come'; **ne ouzon tamm hag echuet o deus** 'I don't know at all whether they have finished'.

SYNTAX

WORD ORDER

197. Provided that the rules given above are observed, especially as far as the verbal particles and the conjunctions are concerned, words can usually be placed in the sentence in any order.

Breton syntax is very free in this respect.

INTERROGATION

198. Interrogative phrases do not differ from others, except of course those which contain an interrogative word. In the spoken language, intonation suffices to make the difference between an interrogative and a declarative sentence known. In the written language, one has recourse to the question mark: Examples: **dont a rit** 'you come'; **dont a rit?** 'are you coming?'

199. Sometimes, however, interrogative sentences are preceded by **ha**, or, if one wishes to stress them, by **daoust ha**. Examples: **ha klañv eo?** 'is he ill?'; **daoust ha klañv eo?** 'is it that he's ill?'

THE RELATIVE

200. Breton has a relative pronoun **a**, which is used when the antecedent is subject or direct object of the subordinate clause: **an den a gerzh** 'the person who walks'; **an den a welan** 'the person whom I see'.

Note: This *a* is the verbal particle. Context alone permits one to distinguish whether a sentence like *an den a gerzh* means 'the person walks' or 'the person who walks'.

201. In the spoken language **a** is often preceded by **hag**: **an den hag a gerzh**, **an den hag a welan**, when the idea of the relativity is to be stressed. To stress it even more strongly, one may say **a gement a**. Example: **an den a gement a gerzh**.

202. When the antecedent is neither subject nor direct object, a special expression is used, in which a conjugated preposition is placed at the end

65

of the subordinate clause: **an den a gomzan anezhañ** 'the person of whom I speak', lit. 'the person that I speak of him'.

203. In this case, **a** is often replaced by **ma**, and sometimes by the verbal particle **e**. Example: **an den ma komzan anezhañ**.

Note: The relative pronoun *where*, in the sense of 'in which' offers likewise no difficulty. For example 'the country where he built his house" is expressed: *ar vro a savas e di enni* lit. 'the country that he built his house in it', or even *ar vro ma savas e di enni*.

One may otherwise express 'where' simply by *ma*. Example: *ar vro ma savas e di* 'the country where he built his house'.

This is also true when the relative is *when*, in the sense of 'on which'. Example: *an deiz' ma skrive* 'the day when he was writing'.

204. When the verb of the subordinate clause is in the negative, the relative pronoun **a** is replaced by **na**. Examples: **an den na gerzh ket** 'the person who doesn't walk'; **an den na welan ket** 'the person whom I don't see'; **an den na gomzan ket anezhañ** 'the person about whom I do not speak'.

Note I: A remark analogous to that made at §195 may be made here. It is possible to use *ma* before *ne*. Examples: *an den ma ne gomzan ket anezhañ* 'the person of whom I do not speak'; *an deiz' ma ne skrive ket* 'the day when he was not writing'.

Note II: In speech the *na* is often omitted: *un den 'gerzh ket*. This does not occur when *na* precedes a vowel: *an den n'ouzon ket pelec'h emañ*.

205. The relative pronoun **a** is omitted like the verbal particle **a**. See §§167 and 168.

The Pronunciation of Breton

GENERAL

206. Although the Breton dialects differ from one another somewhat as regards pronunciation, they have more in common than would divide them.

207. Since Unified Breton (*brezhoneg peurunvan*) has been fixed as a written standard, it is here taken as a base for fixing a spoken standard. Unified Breton has sometimes been called *ar zedacheg*, because it writes with *zh* sounds which in some dialects are pronounced [z] and in others [x].

208. Four main dialects are generally recognized in Breton, indicated on the frontispiece map on page ii. Broadly speaking, Kerneveg, Leoneg, and Tregerieg (KLT) have more in common with one another than they have with Gwenedeg, though this is an oversimplification. Leoneg, for instance has several features not shared by the other dialects, such as the tendency to pronounce **-z'-** where other dialects have lost it. To the foreign ear, the the most noticeable feature of Gwenedeg is the use of [c] and [ɟ] in place of [k] and [g] before front vowels.

209. This is not a complete and detailed tableau of any particular dialect. Rather, it is a simple, schematized picture of the phonetic outline of the language. Nevertheless, in this sketch the important Gwenedeg forms have been given as an aid to the learner.

210. An attempt has been made, as far as is possible, to make this discussion intelligible to readers who have no special knowledge of phonetics.

211. Finally, reference is often made to the pronunciation of Breton *vis à vis* that of French, the assumption being that all readers are familiar with that. Those who do not should refer to works on the pronunciation of French.

GRAPHIC REPRESENTATION

212. It is customary in phonetic works to employ a special notation to represent sounds. This is done because the resources of ordinary orthography, whether English or French, are imperfect.

213. The notation of the International Phonetic Association is used here.

214. The phonetic alphabet is given below; after each letter an example is given from English (or from other languages when the corresponding sound does not exist in English).

IPA	Examples
a	Fr. m**a**l, approx. Eng. b**u**y [baɪ], n**o**w [naʊ]
ɑ	Fr. p**a**s, approx. Eng. f**a**ther [fɑːðɚ]
b	Eng. **b**oat
c	more palatalized than Eng. **ch**ip [tʃɪp]
ç	palatalized [x], as in Ger. ni**ch**t, Eng. dialect **h**uman
d	Eng. **d**ote or **d**ill
e	approx. Fr. **été**, N. Eng. s**a**te
ə	Eng. **a**bout
ɛ	approx. Fr. tr**è**s or Eng. s**e**t (allophonic variant [ɛ̞] is more open still, see §230)
f	approx. Eng. **f**ight
ɡ	approx Eng. **g**oat or **g**ill
ɣ	Irish **dh**á, N. Ger. sa**g**en
h	Eng. **h**ack (or **h**onour) (see §238)
ɦ	voiced [h]
i	approx. Eng. mach**i**ne
j	Eng. **y**ak
ɟ	more palatalized than Eng. **j**u**dg**e [dʒʌdʒ]
k	approx. Eng. **c**oat or **k**ill
l	approx. Eng. **l**ack (allophonic variant [ɬ] is voiceless as Welsh **ll**an)
ʎ	Span. **ll**ano, Ital. de**gl**i; approx. Eng. mi**lli**on
m	Eng. **m**ote
n	Eng. **n**ote
ɲ	Fr. ga**gn**e, Span. a**ñ**o; approx. Eng. o**ni**on

ŋ	Eng. si**ng**
o	approx. Fr. s**o**t, Eng. s**o**ap
ɔ	approx. Fr. s**o**tte, Eng. s**o**p (allophonic variant [ɒ] is more open still, see §230)
ø	approx. Fr. p**eu**, Ger. H**öh**le
œ	approx. Fr. **œu**vre, Ger. H**ö**lle (allophonic variant [œ̞] is more open still, see §230)
p	Eng. **p**ack
r	Span. pe**r**o; approx. American la**dd**er
ʁ	Fr. **r**i**r**e, Ger. **r**ichtig (allophonic [χ] is voiceless)
s	Eng. **s**ack
ʃ	Eng. **sh**ack
t	approx. Eng. **t**ote or **t**ill
u	approx. Eng t**oo**
ɥ	Fr. n**u**it
v	approx. Eng. **v**ote
w	Eng. **w**oke or **w**in
x	Irish na**ch**, Ger. na**ch**
y	Fr. **u**ne, Ger. gr**ü**n
z	Eng. **z**one
ʒ	Eng. mea**s**ure

215. A tilde over a vowel indicates that it is nasalized.

IPA	Examples
ã	Breton sk**añ**v 'light'; approx. Fr. cr**an** [kʁã]
ɛ̃	Breton kr**eñ**v 'strong'; not very like Fr. f**in** [fɛ̃]
ĩ	Breton b**iñ**s 'screw'
õ	Breton p**on**t 'bridge'; approx. Fr. m**on** [mɔ̃]
œ̃	Breton bl**euñ**v 'flowers'; approx Fr. br**un** [bʁœ̃]
ỹ	Breton p**uñ**s 'well'

216. A long vowel is represented by following it with two points; thus [ɑː] means 'long ɑ'.

217. Tonic accent is represented by a stroke before the stressed syllable: **bara** 'bread' [ˈbɑːʁa].

218. Phonetic representations are given within square brackets.

CONSONANTS

219. When a consonant is pronounced, the vocal cords, situated in the larynx, may vibrate (voiced consonants) or not (voiceless consonants). The distinctive sound of the consonant is produced by the air escaping from the lungs against an obstruction formed by the closure or restriction of a point (or a number of points) between the vocal cords and the lips.

The voiced consonants of Breton are:

[b d ɟ g m n ɲ ŋ l ʎ ʁ v r ʒ ɣ ɦ w ɥ z j].

The voiceless ones are: [p t c k ç f ʃ x h s].

Consonants are classified according to the point of articulation as:

a) bilabial (between the two lips): [p b m w ɥ];

b) labiodental (bottom lip against the top teeth): [f v];

c) apico-dental (between the front of the palate and the end of the tongue): [t d n l r s z ʃ ʒ];

d) palatal (between the middle of the palate and the middle of the tongue): [c ɟ ɲ ʎ ç j];

e) velar (between the back of the palate and the back of the tongue): [k g ŋ x ɣ];

f) uvular (in the throat): [ʁ];

g) glottal (between the vocal cords): [h ɦ].

The manner of articulation further distinguishes consonants as:

1)	stops	[p b t d c ɟ k g]
2)	nasals	[m n ɲ ŋ]
3)	laterals	[l ʎ]
4)	rolled	[r ʁ]
5)	fricatives	[f v s z ʃ ʒ ç x ɣ h ɦ]
6)	semivowels	[w ɥ j]

Note: Some scholars assert that the chief opposition in the Breton consonantal system is not *voice* vs. *voicelessness*, but rather *lenis* vs. *fortis*, i.e., the strength with which they are articulated. Briefly, consonants written as voiced are weaker and shorter than those written as voiceless—this has the acoustic effect of sounding like a voiced-voiceless distinction to speakers of English, Irish, or Welsh (but cf. the voiceless aspirated vs. voiceless nonaspirated distinction in Danish, and the three grades of short (lenis), long (fortis), and overlong (long fortis), voiceless consonants in Estonian). Both fortis and lenis consonants have a tendency to neutralize to devoiced lenes in absolute final position (see §251 below); the product of a fortis and a lenis in contact will follow approximately the rules given as for voiceless and voiced in §§252–54 below).

It has not been considered practical to demonstrate this difference in a grammar with the limited scope of this one; and the voiced-voiceless distinction will serve the learner adequately until he or she encounters Breton first-hand. For further discussion of this question see Press 1986, Kervella 1976, and Jackson 1967.

220. Stops or occlusives are obtained when the passage of air is closed at a given point, and then opened suddenly. Before a stressed vowel, the voiceless [p], [t], and [k] are aspirated somewhat more strongly than in French, being rather more like English consonants: **pegañ** 'glue' ['pe:gã]; **tachenn** 'plot of land' ['taʃɛn]; **kador** 'chair' ['kɑ:dɔʁ].

221. Nasals are obtained like occlusives, with the difference that the velum or soft palate is lowered, allowing some of the air coming from the lungs to escape through the nostrils. Breton [ɲ] has no equivalent in English. The middle of the tongue presses against the middle of the palate; it is written *ñ* in Spanish, *ny* in Catalan, *gn* in French and Italian: **kignen** 'garlic' ['kiɲɛn]/[ciɲen]; **ognon** 'onions' ['õɲõn]; **gagn** 'carrion' [gãɲ]. This sound is a bit different from that in English *onion* ['ʌnjɔn].

222. Laterals are obtained when the passage of air is almost closed with the tongue, so that it can escape by the sides only, often by a single side.

In the pronunciation of [l], the tip of the tongue closes the passage. In the pronunciation of Breton [l], the middle of the tongue is lowered in general more than in French. This is most obvious in final position, after a short stressed vowel: **koll** 'lose' [kɔl], **dall** 'blind' [dal]. Compare English *mill, tell.*

After a voiceless consonant, the Breton [l] sometimes allophonically devoices as French [l] does in the same position one can represent this voiceless [l] by [ɬ]. Compare **riskl** 'danger' [ʁiskɬ] and French *cycle* [sikɬ]. This is similar to the sound found in Welsh *Llan* [ɬan] or sometimes, allophonically, in heavily aspirated English *plan!* ['pʰɬæːn].

[ʎ] has no equivalent in English. The middle of the tongue presses against the middle of the palate; it is written *ll* in Spanish, *ly* in Catalan, *gl* in Italian: **dilhad** 'clothes' ['diʎat]; **ruilhet** 'rolled' ['ʁyʎet]; **sailh** 'bucket' [saʎ]; **boutailh** 'bottle' ['butaʎ]; **spilhenn** 'pin' ['spiʎɛn]. This sound is close to, but not identical to that in English *million* ['mɪljɔn]. Many

Bretons replace [ʎ] with [j]. The preceding words become ['dijɔt], ['ʁyjet], [saj], ['butaj], ['spijɔn].

223. r has two main pronunciations. The "rolled" or apical trill [r] is obtained by bringing the point of the tongue near the gums behind the teeth of the upper jaw. The air passing by produces a series of vibrations, a sort of rolling, for which the consonant is named. This is the sound found in Italian, Scottish Gaelic, Spanish, and Welsh. The apical trill [r] is found mostly among older speakers of Leoneg. A similar apical flap [ɾ] (more a tap than a roll) is used by older speakers of Tregerieg; younger speakers of Tregerieg tend to use a retroflex approximant [ɻ].

Elsewhere in Brittany, the "gutteral" or uvular trill [ʁ] is more common. In this case, it is the uvula, at the back of the soft palate, which vibrates against the back of the tongue. This consonant is represented by [ʁ]. This is the sound found in standard French and German. In parts of Central Brittany a voiceless version of this sound, a post-velar or uvular fricative [χ], is used. The [ʁ] is the sound used in Kerneveg and in the standard language.

Learners who speak French or German may as well use the back [ʁ]; Welsh and Scottish learners with [r], however, may feel free to use that sound. Since it is more common, [ʁ] is written here.

After a voiceless consonant, [r] and [ʁ] devoice to [r̥] and [χ] under the same conditions as [l] (see §222) in Breton as in French. Compare **mestr** 'master' [mɛstr̥] or [mɛstχ] and *équestre* [e'kɛstr̥] or [e'kɛstχ]. Note that [mɛst] is heard far more often than either of these.

224. Fricatives are the consonants obtained by restricting the passage of air in a given place, which produces a sort of friction.

[h] is identical to the English [h] in *house*. See §238.

[x] has no equivalent in English. It is articulated between the back of the palate and the back of the tongue. It corresponds to the Irish or German [x], written *ch*, in *nach*: **marc'h** 'horse' [maʁx]; **yac'h** 'healthy' [ja:x]; **c'hwitellit** 'you whistle' [xwi'tɛlit]/['ɥitɛlit]; **mousc'hoarzh** 'smile' ['musxwaʁs]/['mushwaʁx]. In Leoneg it can sometimes be voiced to [ɦ] or [ɣ] **c'hoazh** 'already' [ɣwa:s]/[ɦwa:s] (Gwenedeg [hwa:x] or [wa:x]), **yac'hus** 'healthy' ['jaɦys] (but not in comparatives and superlatives: **yac'hoc'h** 'healthiest' ['jaxɔx].

The consonants [f] and [v] in Breton usually have labio-dental articulation as in English (between the teeth of the upper jaw and the lower lip): **falz** 'sickle' [fals]; **avel** 'wind' ['aːvɛl]. In many dialects [w] is used instead of [v].

Note I: The strengthening which the comparative and superlative endings -*añ* and -*oc'h* give to -*c'h*- in *yac'hoc'h* here is extended to other consonants; this is sometimes reflected in the orthography as noted at §75 above.

Note II: In the area of Central Brittany where /r/ is realized as voiceless uvular [χ], /x/ is realized as pharyngeal [ħ].

Note III: In Leoneg orthographic -*z*- is always pronounced. In other dialects, however, it is sometimes pronounced and sometimes not. In this book -*z'*- is used to mark the unpronounced one: *gwaz'* 'goose' is written [ɡwɑː(s)] here (Lagadeg & Menard 1995 write [ɡ°ɑː(s)]), *ruz'iañ* 'redden' is written ['ʁy(z)jã] here (Lagadeg & Menard write ['ʁyʃːã] (or ['ʁyzjã]) for Leoneg and ['ʁyjːã] for Tregerieg and Kerneveg).

225. Semivowels are sonants that have the same articulatory position as certain vowels, [w] as [u], [ɥ] as [y], [j] as [i], with the difference that the passage of air is restricted more strongly than for the vowel. They are the same in Breton as in French: **gwad** 'blood' [ɡwɑːt]; **mui** 'more' [mɥi]; **reier** 'rocks' ['ʁɛjɛʁ]. Compare the French *boite* [bwat]; *nuit* [nɥi]; *rivière* [ʁiˈvjɛʁ].

VOWELS

226. When a vowel is pronounced, the vocal cords always vibrate; the restriction of the air passage is not sufficient to produce a sound, as in the case of a consonant; the distinctive sound is produced only by the resonance of the mouth cavity.

The Breton vowels may be classed thus:

	Front	Rounded	Back	
high	i	y	u	
high mid	e	ø	o	closed
mid	ɛ	œ	ɔ	open
low	a		ɑ	

QUANTITY

227. Every unstressed vowel is short. A stressed vowel is short when it is followed:

a) by another vowel or semivowel: **aotrou** 'mister' ['awtʁu] (or ['otʁu]); **kleiz'** 'chalk' [klɛi(s)]; **moal** 'bald' ['mɔɑːl] (or [mwɑːl]); **kaier** 'notebook' ['kajɛʁ]; **diwall** 'protect' ['diwal].

b) by a voiceless consonant [p t k f ʃ s x]: **strap** 'crash' [stʁap]; **ket** 'not' [ket]/[cet]; **stok** 'contact' [stok]; **stouf** 'cork' [stuf]; **sachañ** 'drag' ['saʃã]; **kas** 'send' [kas]; **loc'h** 'lake' [lox].

c) by consonant clusters: **park** 'field' [paʁk]; **marc'h** 'horse' [maʁx]; **falz** 'sickle' [fals]; **kelc'h** 'circle' [kɛlx]/[cɛlx]; **skolioù** 'schools' ['skolju] (cf. **skol** [skoːl]).

d) by nasals and liquids [m n ɲ l ʎ ʁ]: **prim** 'quick' [pʁim]; **tomm** 'shaft, trunk' [tɔm]; **penn** 'head' [pɛn]; **hent** 'way, path' [hɛ̃nt]; **pignat** 'climb' ['piɲat]; **dall** 'blind' [dal]; **gwellañ** 'better' ['gwɛlã]/['ɟɥɛlã]; **spilhoù** 'pins' ['spiʎu]; **berrek** 'short, poor' ['bɛʁɛk]; **torret** 'broken' ['tɔʁet]; **kirri** 'cars' ['kiʁi]/['ciʁi]. Observe that the spelling generally indicates short vowels by writing these consonants double: **nn**, **mm**, **ll**: **lennet** 'read' ['lɛnet]; **mamm** 'mother' [mãm]; **fall** 'bad' [fal]; but that monosyllabic words in **-rr** are generally long: **berr** 'short' [bɛːʁ]; **torr** 'broken; fracture' [tɔːʁ]; **karr** 'car' [kɑːʁ].

228. Many stressed vowels are long. A stressed vowel is long in final position: **ti** 'house' [tiː]; or when it is followed:

a) by a voiced consonant [b d g v ʒ z]: **mab** 'son' [mɑːb]; **lodenn** 'part' ['loːdɛn]; **bag** 'boat' [bɑːg]; **savet** 'risen' ['saːvet]; **nijal** 'fly' ['niːʒal]; **louz** 'guard' [luːz].

> *Note:* The vowels are always long in *mab, bag,* and *louz,* even though the consonant is devoiced in absolute final position (cf. §251). In actual transcription these three would be written [mɑːp], [bɑːk], and [luːs].

b) by consonant clusters ending in **-r** or **-l**: **pebr** 'pepper' [peːbʁ] (but usually [pep]); **sukr** 'sugar' [syːkχ]/[syːkr̩] (usually [syk]); **konikled** 'rabbits' [kõˈniːklet]; **semplañ** 'faint' ['sɛ̃ːmplã] (cf. **semplaat** [sɛ̃mˈplɑːt] with stress shift). (But not those beginning in **-s-**: **lestr** 'dish' [lɛst(ʁ)].)

c) by nasals and liquids [n l ʁ]: **den** 'person' [dẽːn]; (short with following **-j-**: **bleunioù** 'flowers' ['blõnju]; **peul** 'pillar' [pøːl]; **stur** 'rudder' [styːʁ]. See note on spelling in §227.d above.

QUALITY

229. High vowels do not differ appreciably in quality whether short or long. Thus: **poulloù** 'pools' ['pulu] and **trouz** 'pools' [tʁuːs]; **lusk** 'impetus' [lysk] and **lur** 'pools' [lyːʁ]; **kirri** 'cars' ['kiʁi]/['ciʁi] and **gwir** 'true' [gwiːʁ]/[ɥiːʁ].

230. Mid-vowels have three qualities: closed, open, and very open.

a) Mid-vowels are closed when long: **beg** 'beak' [beːk]; **hed** 'length' [heːt]; **den** 'person' [dẽːn]; **mel** 'honey' [meːl]; **bez'** 'grave' [beː(s)]; **dor** 'door' [doːʁ]; **kozh** 'old' [koːs]; **moged** 'smoke' ['moːget]; **bleunioù** 'flowers' ['blõnju]; **peul** 'pillar' [pøːl]; **leur** 'floor' [løːʁ]. **e** can be closed when short in some words: **hep** 'without' [hep]; **pesk** 'fish' [pesk]; **Brest** 'Brest' [bʁest]; **spes** 'appearance' [spes]; **tech** 'tendency' [teʃ].

b) Mid-vowels are open when unstressed, as in suffixes (mostly in Leoneg): **karet** 'loved' ['kɑːʁɛt] (elsewhere ['kɑːʁet]); **lanneg** 'heath' ['lãnɛk]; **kilhog** 'cock' ['kiʎɔk]/['ciʎok]; **gwelloc'h** 'best' ['gwɛlɔx]/['ɥɥɛlox]. They tend to close again when stress shifts to them with the addition of a second suffix (see §268): **karetoc'h** 'most loved' [kɑːˈʁetɔx]; **lanneier** 'heaths' [lãˈnejɛʁ].

c)   Mid-vowels are very open before [lx], [ʁx] (less often before [x]), the semivowels [y] or [w], or before other clusters beginning with -l- or -r-, and sometimes -rr-: **kelc'h** 'circle' [kɛlx]/[cɛlx]; **merc'h** 'daughter' [mɛʁx]; **sec'h** 'dry' [sɛx] (but also [sex]); **eien** 'source' ['ɛjɛn] (also ['ejɛn]); **nerzh** 'strength' [nɛʁs]/[nɛʁx]; **nervenn** 'nerve' ['nɛʁvɛn]; **terriñ** 'break' ['tɛʁĩ]; **n'oc'h ket** 'you are not' ['nɔx 'ket]/['nɔx cet]; **roc'h** 'rock' [ʁɔx] (also [ʁox]); **bolc'h** 'husk, pod' [bɔlx]; **lorc'h** 'pride' [lɔʁx]; **tort** 'hump' [tɔʁt]; **torzh** 'loaf' [tɔʁs]/[tɔʁx]; **horjellañ** 'wobble' [hɔʁ'ʒɛlã] (but **horellañ** 'wobble' [ho'ʁɛlã]); **skoliañ** 'teach' ['skɔljã]; **teuc'h** 'second-hand (clothes); obese' [tœx] (also [tøx]); **cheulk** 'churl' [ʃœlk]; **seurt** 'sort' [sœʁt].

Note I: It appears that there are only five mid-vowel phonemes in Breton, namely [e ɛ o ɔ ø]; very open [ɛ̞ ɔ̞] and both open and very open [œ œ̞] seem to be predictably conditioned allophones of [ɛ ɔ ø].

Note II: In endings like **-enn** and **-erezh**, both [ɛn]/[ən] and [e:ʁes]/[ɛ:ʁes] are found; in many cases, such as in the past participle ending **-et**, [et]/[ət] are found. Unstressed **e** is often pronounced [ə].

231. The low vowel has two qualities:

a)   **a** is closed when long in a monosyllable: **stag** 'link' [stɑ:k]; **had** 'seed' [hɑ:t]; **tal** 'forehead' [tɑ:l]; **kazh** 'cat' [kɑ:s]/[kɑ:x].

b)   **a** is open when short: **dall** 'blind' [dal]; **marc'h** 'horse' [maʁx]; **tach** 'nail' [taʃ].

232. Breton long vowels are strongly stressed from the beginning to the end, and they tend to close while they are held.

NASAL VOWELS

233. In Breton, any vowel can be nasalized, though in standard French only four vowels [ɑ ɛ ɔ œ] can be nasalized: *tant* [tɑ̃], *brin* [bʁɛ̃], *long* [lɔ̃], *brun* [bʁœ̃].

Some examples: **evitañ** 'for him' [e'vitã]/[(e)ɥitã]; **biñs** 'screw' [bĩs]; **kreñv** 'strong' [kʁẽ(v)]/[kʁẽw]; **heñvel** 'similar' ['hẽ:vel]; **skañv** 'bench' ['skãw]; **bleuñv** 'flowers' [blø̃:]/[blẽw]; **puñs** 'well' [pỹ:s].

234. Before nasal consonants [m n ɲ ŋ], the Breton vowels have a tendency to nasalize. This is particularly apparent for [a o a: o: ø: e:]: **fank** 'mud' [fãŋk]; **evidomp** 'for us' [vi'dom(p)]; **kanañ** 'sing' ['kã:nã]; **kalonek** 'courageous' [ka'lõ:nek]; **leun** 'full' [lø̃:n]; **den** 'person' [dẽ:n].

FROM SPELLING TO PRONUNCIATION

235. Breton spelling, with the exception of what will be said about the voicing and devoicing of stops and spirants below (§§250–54), represents most often each sound in a single and unique way. Each letter (or group of letters such as **ch**, **gn**, **c'h**, etc.) generally corresponds respectively to a single sound. The exceptions are indicated here.

236. In certain regions there is a tendency to pronounce **c'h** as [h] in certain cases. It is clearer to use the stronger [x] in each case. The very strong [ɣ] is found chiefly in northern Brittany.

237. **i** is usually pronounced [i]; but before a vowel, it is generally [j]: **livioù** 'colours' ['livju]; the exceptions are **liorzh** 'garden' ['li:ɔʁs]/['li:ɔʁx]; **lien** 'linen' ['li:ɛn].

238. The letter **h** is aspirated as in English; in Leon and Eastern Gwened the **h** is silent: **heol** 'sun' ['hɛɔl]/['ɛɔl]; **hir** 'long' [hi:ʁ]/[i:ʁ]; **hemañ** 'this one' ['hemã(n)]/['emã(n)].
The letter **h** is *never* sounded in the words **ha**, **hag** 'and'; **he**, **hec'h** 'her, hers'; **ho**, **hoc'h** 'your'; **holl** 'all'; **hon**, **hor**, **hol** 'our', where it is purely orthographic.

239. **lh** represents [ʎ] after **i**: **dilhad** 'clothes' ['diʎat]; but after another vowel, [ʎ] is represented by **ilh**: **sailh** 'bucket' [saʎ]; **skuilhañ** 'spill' ['skyʎã]/['scyʎã].

240. **n** before **k** or **g** represents [ŋ]: **rankout** 'should' ['ʁãŋkut]; **angell** 'fin' ['ãŋgɛl].

241. **o** generally represents [o]; but before a vowel it represents almost always [w]: **c'hoar** 'sister' [xwɑ:ʁ]/[hwɑ:ʁ]; **loer** 'sock' [lwɛ:ʁ]. One can also say ['xɔɑ:ʁ], ['lɔɛ:ʁ].

242. **ou** generally represents [u]; but before a vowel it represents almost always [w]: **gouez'** 'wild' [gwe:(s)]; **gouelañ** 'to weep' ['gwe:lã]; **laouen** 'joyous' ['lɔwɛn]. Exceptions are: **Doue** 'God' ['du:e]; **douar** 'earth' ['du:aʁ]; **gouarn** 'govern' ['gu:aʁn] but also ['gwaʁn].

243. sh is pronounced [s], **zh** is pronounced [z]. In Gwenedeg, **sh** and **zh** are pronounced [x]. **sk** is pronounced [sk]. In Gwenedeg, **sk** is pronounced [sc] or [ʃc] before front vowels and **st** is always [ʃt].

244. u is generally pronounced [y]; in the words **mui** 'more', **skuizh** 'tired', **kuit** 'away, departed', and the words derived from them, **u** is pronounced [ɥ]: [mɥiː], [skɥiːs]/[scɥiːx], [kɥit]/[cɥit].

245. v is generally pronounced [v]; but in final position it is often pronounced [ɔ], [w], or [ɥ], except:
a) in verbs: **ev ar gwin-mañ** 'drink this wine' [ˈeːv aʁ ˈgwiːn mã]/[ˈeːv aʁ ɥiːn mã]
b) after **ñ**: **skañv eo** 'it is easy' [ˈskãːv eɔ]/[ˈskãːv eː]
In the words **bliv** 'quick', **div** 'two' **Gwiskriv** 'Guiscriff', **gwiv** 'merry', **liv** 'colour', **piv** 'who', **riv** 'cold', **v** is pronounced [u]; in Gwenedeg, **v** is pronounced [ɥ] most of the time: [ˈbliu]/[ˈbliɥ], [ˈdiu]/[ˈdiɥ], [ˈgwiskʁiu]/[ɥiskʁiɥ], [ˈgwiu]/[ɥiɥ], [ˈliu]/[ˈliɥ], [ˈpiu]/[ˈpiɥ], [ˈʁiu]/[ˈʁiɥ]. In the Goelo dialect this **v** is [f]: **piv** is [pif].

246. y is pronounced [j] before a vowel and in final position: **yar** 'chicken' [jɑːʁ]; **yod** 'porridge' [joːt]; **ay** 'will go' [ˈaj]; **gray** 'will do' [ˈgʁaj]; **roy** 'will give' [ˈʁoj]; **lakay** 'will put' [ˈlakaj]; **nay** 'fool' [ˈnaj].

247. The digraph **eu** represents [ø] or [œ] and the digraph **ou** represents [u]. A diaeresis ¨ is placed over the **u** to indicate when it is pronounced [ey] or [oy]: **eürus** 'happy' [ˈɛyʁys] (also [eˈ(v)yːʁys]), **emroüs** 'devoted' [ɛmˈʁoːys].

248. The words **stêr** 'river', **hêr** 'heir', and **kêr** 'town', are written with the circumflex ^ to distinguish them from their homonyms **ster** 'sense', **her** 'bold', and **ker** 'dear' [stɛːʁ], [hɛːʁ], [kɛːʁ]. The circumflex accent is found in the derived words from these as well. A circumflex is also placed on the **o** on **trôad** 'circuit, tour' [ˈtʁoːat] to distinguish it from **troad** 'foot' [ˈtʁwɑːt]. The vocative particle is also sometimes written with a circumflex: **â Vreizh!** 'o Brittany!'.

249. The grave accent ` placed on the **u** of the plural ending **où** indicates that one can pronounce it (ranging geographically from Northwest Leon to Southeast Gwened) [u], [o], [ø], [ow], [aw], [aɥ], or [ɔɥ].

MODIFICATION OF SOUNDS

250. The spelling does not take into account certain sound modifications at the end of words. When ['bɛːlɛk] is given as phonetic transcription of a word written **beleg** 'priest', this does not exclude the pronunciation ['bɛːlɛg] in certain contexts.

Note: See the Note at §219 above.

251. The rule is very simple. It affects seven voiceless consonants and seven voiced ones:

voiceless: [p t k f ʃ x s]
voiced: [b d g v ʒ ɣ z]

These are called interchangeable consonants, for the same word can, depending on its environment, end in [p] or in [b], as in the examples below; in [t] or in [d], in [k] or in [g], etc.

At the end of a word, the voiceless consonant is always pronounced, unless the following word begins with a voiced one (on the condition, of course, that there is no break between the two words).

Therefore one says: **sellit ouzh ar beleg** 'look at the priest' ['sɛlid uz aʁ 'bɛːlɛk]; **setu amañ ar beleg kozh** 'here is the old priest' ['sety 'ãmã aʁ 'bɛːlɛk 'koːs]; **beleg ar barrez** 'the priest of the parish' ['bɛːlɛg aʁ 'baʁes]; **ur beleg mat** 'a good priest' [œʁ 'bɛːlɛg 'maːt]; **ur beleg mat eo** 'He is a good priest' [œʁ 'bɛːlɛg 'maːd eɔ]/[œʁ 'bɛːlɛg 'maːd eː].

Note: See the Note at §219 above.

252. The rule has only one important exception: the result of the combination of two identical or corresponding interchangeable consonants is always voiceless, even if the second is voiced: **bloaz' 'zo** 'a year ago' ['blwa(s) 'so]; **dek gwele** 'ten beds' ['deːk 'kweːle].

Note I: This is a very important feature of Breton. Even in Gwenedeg dialects in which *bloaz'* is pronounced [bleː], this feature is maintained and ['bleː 'so] is the rule.
Note II: [s] does not voice in some words, especially those of French origin; [ʃ] often resists voicing.

253. The rule can apply to a group of consonants in final position: **klask avaloù** 'look for apples' ['klazg a'va:lu].

254. Finally the rule applies to the interior of a word between consecutive consonants, even if the spelling does not take it into account: **rakdiazez'añ** 'pre-establish' [ʁaqdia'ze:(z)ã]; **addeskiñ** 'relearn' [at'teskĩ].

LOSS OF SOUNDS

255. The phenomena studied here occur whenever one speaks reasonably quickly. The faster one speaks, the more numerous and frequent these modifications are. Only those which occur generally in ordinary conversation are mentioned here.

256. Certain unstressed vowels are often lost. For example:
   a)   in the article: **ti an diaoul** 'the house of the devil' ['ti:n 'djɔwl]
   b)   in adverbs and prepositions beginning with **a** or **e**: **a-raok** 'before' ['ʁɔ:k]; **evel** 'as' [vɛl]
   c)   in the forms of the verb **endevout** 'have': **dour am eus** 'I have water' ['du:ʁ m øs]; **petra ho poa graet?** 'what have you done?' [petʁa: pwa 'gʁɛ:t]
   d)   in the forms of the present of the locative of the verb *to be* (see §149): **amañ emañ** 'he is here' ['ãmã mã]; **aze emaoc'h** 'you are there' ['a:ze mɔx]
   e)   in the words **pelec'h** 'where', **perak** 'why': **pelec'h emaoc'h?** 'where are you?' ['ple:x mɔx]; **perak eo deut** 'why has he come?' ['pʁa:q e 'dø:t]
   f)   in the verbal particles **a, e, ez, ec'h, o, oc'h**: **me a lavar** 'I say' [me 'la:vaʁ] (also [me 'la:ʁ]); **o vont d'ar gêr** 'going home' ['võn daʁ 'gɛ:ʁ]/['võn daʁ 'jɛ:ʁ].

257. Note that an unstressed vowel, without being completely lost, can be reduced to a neutral sound pronounced with the tongue and lips relaxed and more or less distant from the expected position.

258. Loss of consonants occurs frequently in words ending in a group of consonants: **mont** 'go' [mõn]; **kambr** 'room' [kãm(p)]; **kanomp** 'let us sing' ['kã:nɔm]; **paotr** 'boy' ['pot] (also ['pɔ:t]); **mestr** 'master' [mɛst].

259. The final consonant is never lost when the second-to-last consonant of the word is [s ʁ l]: **pesk** 'fish' [pesk]; **start** 'solid' [staʁt]; **kalz** 'many' [kals].

260. When one or more consonants are lost this way, there is compensatory lengthening of the last vowel if it is stressed: **levr** 'book' [levʁ]/[leːf] (also [leɔʁ]/[leːw]); **gopr** 'salary' [gɔpʁ]/[goːp].

261. Phenomena of the same sort can occur within a word: **debrfe** 'will eat' [ˈdeːpfɛ].

262. It is important to note the loss of stops at the end of certain words like **evit** 'for', **ket** 'not', **bet** 'been', especially before a consonant: **evit kanañ** 'for singing' [vi ˈkãːnã]; **ne gan ket mat** 'he doesn't sing well' [ne ˈgãːn ke ˈmɑːt]/[ne ˈgãːn ce ˈmɑːt].

263. The consonant **n** is lost in words like **evidon** 'for me', **ouzhin** 'against me', placed before **me** 'me' when **me** serves to intensify the sense: **evidon-me** [viˈdɔ̃me]; **ouzhin-me** [uˈzĩme].

264. The negative particle **ne** is usually lost: **n-em eus ket** 'I do not have' [m øs ˈket]/[m øs ˈcet]; **ne gan ket mat** 'he doesn't sing well' [ˈgãːn ke ˈmɑːt]/[ˈgãːn ce ˈmɑːt].

265. Note that the facts cited above are not to be considered as dialectal, irregular formations, or faults of pronunciation. They represent the natural and normal pronunciation of everyday conversation.

STRESS ACCENT

266. Stress accent in Breton is very strongly realized.

267. The orthography is taken as a base for describing the rules for stress accent.

STRESS IN THE ISOLATED WORD

268. In a word taken in isolation the stress accent falls generally on the penultimate syllable. A Breton word contains as many syllables as it has vowels or groups of vowels: **kaner** 'singer' ['kã:nɛʁ]. In southern Brittany the distinction between stressed and unstressed syllables is reduced and the stress can occur on the final syllable instead of the pentultimate.

269. In a group of vowels, it is the first which, if it can, receives the stress: **aotre** 'permission' ['aɔtʁe] (also ['otʁe]).

270. This last rule is valid for monosyllables containing a group of vowels: **feiz** 'faith' ['fɛi(s)].

271. It is important to note that the spelling sometimes indicates groups of vowels which are not really there: **gouenn** 'race' [gwɛn]; **foetañ** 'whip' ['fwetã]; **kelien** 'flies' ['kɛljɛn]/['celjõn]; **skuizh** 'tired' [skɥi:s]/[scɥi:x]; **miaoual** 'to miaow/meow' ['mjawal] (but also [mi'ɔwal]); **miaoñval** also exists.

272. Likewise, it is important to distinguish between the groups of vowels proper and the juxtapositions of vowels due to the chance of word composition: **baleadenn** 'walk' [bale'ɑ:dɛn], formed from **bale** and the suffix **-adenn**; **bilienn** 'cobble' [bi'liɛn], from **bili** and the suffix **-enn**.

273. This point established, there remain a great number of exceptions to the rule. In particular, in certain words the stress falls on the last syllable.

Here are the principal examples:
a) nouns: **itron** 'lady', **Pantekost** 'Pentecost', **pemoc'h** 'pig'.
b) an adjective: **fallakr** 'wicked'
c) the forms of the verb **bez'añ** 'be', in the present of the locative (**emaon, emaout, emañ**...)
d) conjugated prepositions: first and second persons, singular and plural, types II.B and II.C in the table of prepositions following

§186. Examples: **ouzhin** 'against me' [uˈzĩn]; **diouzhit** 'from you' [diuˈzit]; **ganimp**, **ganeomp** 'with us' [gãˈnĩmp]/ [gãˈneɔ̃mp]; **diganeoc'h** 'from you' [digaˈneɔx]

e) adverbs, pronouns, prepositions, etc.:

abred 'soon'
ac'han 'from here'
afo 'quickly'
anez 'if not'
antronoz 'the next day'
atav 'always'
avat 'however'
bennak 'some'
bepred 'always'
biskoazh 'never
dalc'hmat 'always'
davet 'toward'
davit 'toward
diabarzh 'interior'
diagent 'before(hand)'
diavaez 'exterior'
dilun 'Monday'
dimeurzh 'Tuesday'
dindan 'under'
diriaou 'Thursday'
diouzhtu 'right away'
disul 'Sunday'
eben 'the other'
ebet 'none'
eget 'that'
emberr 'as soon'
eme 'said'
emichañs 'maybe'
ervat 'well'
eta 'thus'
etre 'between'
evel 'as'
evelkent 'however'
evit 'for'
fenoz 'tonight'
feteiz' 'today'

gwechall 'once, formerly, once upon a time'
hanternoz 'midnight'
hepken 'only'
kenañ 'very'
kenavo 'good bye'
kerkent 'as soon'
kerkoulz 'as well'
kerzu 'December'
kreisteiz' 'noon'
kreiznoz 'midnight'
meurbet 'very'
moarvat 'certainly'
neblec'h 'nowhere'
nemet 'except'
nemetken 'only'
nemeur 'at all'
nepred 'never'
netra 'nothing'
ouzhpenn 'moreover'
padal 'however'
peadra 'enough'
pebezh 'what'
pegeit 'how long'
pegen 'how much'
pegoulz 'when'
pelec'h 'where'
penaos 'how'
peogwir 'because'
perak 'why'
peseurt 'which'
petra 'what'
raktal 'immediately'
trawalc'h 'enough'
warc'hoazh 'tomorrow'
zoken 'even

f) the place names of three syllables beginning with **Kastel-** and of two syllables beginning in **Ker-, Lan-, Log-, Meilh-, Pen-, Plou-, Pon-, Poul-, Tre-** and their variants (**La-, Lo-, Lok-, Lou-, Pel-, Pem-, Peur-, Ple-, Pleur-, Plo-, Pri-, Tri-,** etc.): **Kastellin** 'Châteaulin', **Kerlaz** 'Kerlaz', **Lanmeur** 'Lanmeur', **Lokarn** 'Locarn', **Meilharz',** 'Meilars', **Penharz** 'Penhars', **Pleuveur** 'Pleumeur', **Poulann** 'Poullan', **Trelez** 'Tréflez', etc.

Note that the name **Treger**, Pays de Tréguier, as well as **Landreger**, city of Tréguier, are stressed on the penultimate syllable.

STRESS IN HYPHENATED WORDS

274. When two words are joined by a hyphen, each of them retains its own accentuation: **kabell-touseg** 'mushroom' [ˈkɑːbɛlˈtuːsek].

275. But if the two stresses fall next to one another, the stress of the first word weakens and disappears completely, especially if the compound is in frequent use: **mamm-gozh** 'grandmother' [mãmˈɡoːs]/[mãmˈɡoːx]; **a-walc'h** 'enough' [aˈwalx]; **e-barzh** 'in' [eˈbaʀs]/[baʀx]. **E-barzh** is often pronounced [ba].

276. There is an exception to this last rule for the demonstrative particles **-mañ, -se, -hont**. Theirs is the stress which disappears in cases such as these where two stresses fall together: **an dra-mañ** 'this thing' [ãn ˈdʀɑːmã].

But not always after a preposition: **evel-se** 'like that' [evɛlˈseː].

Note otherwise certain anomalies: **kement-se** 'all that' [keˈmẽn(t) se]/ [keˈmẽ se]; **ar mintin-mañ** 'this morning' [aʀ mĩnˈtĩn mã].

277. When the personal pronouns **me**, **te**, etc., are suffixed by a hyphen to a preposition combined with a personal pronoun, they lose their stress, but move the stress of the preceding word to its last syllable: **evidon-me** 'for me' [eviˈdɔ̃ me].

278. In place names of two syllables beginning with **Sant** 'Saint', the word **Sant** carries the stress: **Sant-Vig** 'Saint-Nic' [ˈsã vik].

PHRASE STRESS

279. Note first of all that the rules given for isolated words apply to all non-hyphenated compounds, whatever their composition: **c'hoarilec'h** 'scene' [xwaˈʀiːlex]; **morvleiz'** 'shark' [ˈmoʀvlɛi(s)]; **daoulin** 'knees' ['dɔwlin]; **dinerzh** 'without strength' ['diːnɛʁs]/[dinɛʁx]. These words are stressed on the penultimate syllable. In other words, prefixes and words which act as prefixes do not alter the rules of stress.

280. There are some words which act as true prefixes, even though they are not written together as compounds with the words they modify. Thus **daou zen** 'two people' is pronounced ['dɔwzẽːn], as if it were written *__daouzen__, in the same way as **daoulin** is pronounced ['dɔwlin].

281. Following is a list of the words which can be considered to be prefixes from the phonetic point of view:
   a)   the indefinite article **un, ur, ul**
   b)   the cardinal adjectives and the word **eil** 'second'
   c)   the words **pet** 'how many', **ken** 'if', **pegen** 'how much', **re** 'too'
   d)   qualicative adjectives before the noun
Examples: **un ti** 'a house' ['œn tiː]; **tregont lur** 'thirty francs' [tʁe'gõn lyːʁ]; **re vras** 'too large' ['ʁeː vʁɑːs]; **ur gwir vab** 'a true son' [œʁ 'gwiːʁ vɑːp]/[œʁ 'gwiːʁ 'ɥiːʁ vɑːp].

SENTENCE STRESS

282. In general, only the principal words of the sentence are stressed: nouns, adjectives, verbs, adverbs, pronouns, and conjugated prepositions. The definite article, possessive adjectives, auxiliary verbs, prepositions, conjunctions, verbal particles, and negative particles do not generally carry stress.

283. But when two stresses occur in juxtaposition to one another, the first stress disappears completely in many cases: **tud vat** 'good people' [tyːd 'vɑːt]; **an ti all** 'the other house' [ãn tiː 'al]; **ne oar ket** 'he doesn't know' [ne waʁ 'ket]/[ne waʁ 'cet].

284. The opposite is the case when the second word is a high-frequency monosyllabic verbal form: **yen eo** 'it is cold' ['jẽːn eɔ]/['jẽːn eː]; **aon am eus** 'I'm afraid' ['ãwn m øs]; **glav a ra** 'it is raining' ['glaw a ʁa].

285. Many influences cause the stress to intensify or to weaken. In the course of a single utterance, it is often the first or the last stress which is the strongest

INTONATION

286. Intonation in Breton is intimately tied to stress: in the course of speaking, it is the stressed syllables which control the elevation and the lowering of the tone.

287. In the majority of cases, every unstressed syllable is pronounced in a lower tone. In the word **keloù** 'news' ['kɛ:lu], the syllable [lu] is generally pronounced in a lower tone than [kɛ:]. This lowering of tone can be detected within the stressed syllable, especially when, as in this example, it contains a long vowel.

288. These two essential rules mark the most striking features of Breton intonation. In other regards, Breton intonation follows rules which are nearly identical to those of French.

BIBLIOGRAPHY

There are many good works on Breton; only a few of these are in English. The following list of books (in English, French, Irish, and Welsh) will be of use to the student:

Andouard, Loeiz, & Éamon Ó Ciosáin
    1987   *Geriadur iwerzhoneg-brezhoneg: gant lavarennoù = Foclóir Gaeilge-Briotáinis: le samplaí.* Lesneven: Mouladurioù Hor Yezh, 1987.
Delaporte, Raymond
    1986   *Elementary Breton-English Dictionary = Geriadurig brezhoneg-saozneg.* Cork: Cork University Press.
    1990   *Elementary English-Breton Dictionary = Geriadurig saozneg-brezhoneg.* Lesneven: Mouladurioù Hor Yezh.
Denez, Pêr
    1980   *Brezhoneg ...buan hag aes: a beginner's course in Breton.* Adapted by Raymond Delaporte. Cork: Cork University Press.
Desbordes, Yann
    1983   *Petite grammaire du breton moderne.* Lesneven: Mouladurioù Hor Yezh.
Deshayes, Albert
    2003   *Dictionnaire étymologique du breton.* Douarnenez: La Chasse-Marée. ISBN 2-9142-0825-3
Faverau, Frañsez
    1992   *Geriadur ar brezhoneg a-vremañ = Dictionnaire du breton contemporain.* Morlaix: Skol Vreizh.
Hemon, Roparz
    1975   *A historical morphology and syntax of Breton.* (Mediaeval and Modern Breton Series; 3) Dublin: Institute for Advanced Studies.
    1975   *Cours élémentaire de breton = Kentelioù brezhoneg eeun.* 8ᵉ édition. Brest: Al Liamm.
    1978   *Nouveau dictionnaire breton-français.* 6ᵉ édition. Brest: Al Liamm.
    1978   *Dictionnaire français-breton.* 6ᵉ édition. Brest: Al Liamm.
    Forthcoming   *Elementary course in Breton = Kentelioù brezhoneg eeun.* Translated, adapted, and revised by Michael Everson. Cathair na Mart: Evertype.
Hincks, Rhisiart
    1991   *Geriadur kembraeg-brezhoneg = Geiriadur Cymraeg-Llydaweg.* Lesneven: Hor Yezh.

Breton Grammar

Jackson, Kenneth Hurlstone
    1967   *A historical phonology of Breton.* Dublin: Institute for Advanced Studies.

Kervella, Frañsez
    1975   *Yezhadur bras ar brezhoneg.* Brest: Al Liamm.
    1984   *Nouvelle méthode de breton.* Rennes: Ouest-France.

Lagadeg, Jean-Yves, & Martial Menard (eds.)
    1995   *Geriadur brezhoneg: gant skouerioù ha skeudennoù.* Ar Releg-Kerhuon: An Here.

Press, Ian
    1986   *A grammar of modern Breton.* (Mouton Grammar Library; 2) Berlin: Mouton.

Stéphan, Laurent, & Visant Sèité
    1984   *Lexique breton-français et français-breton = Geriadurig brezhoneg-galleg ha galleg-brezhoneg.* 20. ed. Bannalec: Emgleo-Breiz.

Trépos, Pierre
    1980   *Grammaire bretonne.* Rennes: Ouest-France.

Vallée, Frañsez
    1980   *Geriadur bras galleg-brezhoneg.* Gronwel: Association bretonne de culture.

Williams, Rita
    1984   *Geriadur brezhonek-kembraek.* Lesneven: Mouladurioù Hor Yezh.

CPSIA information can be obtained
at www.ICGtesting.com
Printed in the USA
BVOW08s2135080917
494282BV00001B/65/P